TREASURY OF LITERATURE

ALL KINDS OF FRIENDS

SENIOR AUTHORS
ROGER C. FARR
DOROTHY S. STRICKLAND

AUTHORS
RICHARD F. ABRAHAMSON
ELLEN BOOTH CHURCH
BARBARA BOWEN COULTER
BERNICE E. CULLINAN
MARGARET A. GALLEGO
W. DORSEY HAMMOND
JUDITH L. IRVIN
KAREN KUTIPER
DONNA M. OGLE
TIMOTHY SHANAHAN
PATRICIA SMITH
JUNKO YOKOTA
HALLIE KAY YOPP

SENIOR CONSULTANTS
ASA G. HILLIARD III
JUDY M. WALLIS

CONSULTANTS
ALONZO A. CRIM
ROLANDO R. HINOJOSA-SMITH
LEE BENNETT HOPKINS
ROBERT J. STERNBERG

HARCOURT BRACE & COMPANY
Orlando Atlanta Austin Boston San Francisco Chicago Dallas New York
Toronto London

ISBN 0-15-301252-8

1 2 3 4 5 6 7 8 9 10   032 97 96 95 94

Acknowledgments

For permission to reprint copyrighted material, grateful acknowledgment is made to the following sources:

Bradbury Press, an Affiliate of Macmillan, Inc.: *The Little Painter of Sabana Grande* by Patricia Maloney Markun, illustrated by Robert Casilla. Text copyright © 1993 by Patricia Maloney Markun; illustrations copyright © 1993 by Robert Casilla.

Carolrhoda Books, Inc., Minneapolis, MN: Cover illustration by Kerry Argent from *Derek the Knitting Dinosaur* by Mary Blackwood. Illustration copyright © 1987 by Kerry Argent. Published in the U.S. in 1990 by Carolrhoda Books, Inc.

Children's Book Press: Cover illustration from *Family Pictures* by Carmen Lomas Garza. Copyright © 1990 by Carmen Lomas Garza. Cover illustration by Fernando Olivera from *The Woman Who Outshone the Sun* by Rosalma Zubizarreta, Harriet Rohmer, and David Schecter. Illustration copyright © 1991 by Fernando Olivera.

Crown Publishers, Inc.: Cover illustration from *Stop That Noise!* by Paul Geraghty. Copyright © 1992 by Paul Geraghty.

Dial Books for Young Readers, a division of Penguin Books USA Inc.: From *Snakey Riddles* by Katy Hall and Lisa Eisenberg, illustrated by Simms Taback. Text copyright © 1990 by Katy Hall and Lisa Eisenberg; illustrations copyright © 1990 by Simms Taback. *The Day Jimmy's Boa Ate the Wash* by Trinka Hakes Noble, illustrated by Steven Kellogg. Text copyright © 1980 by Trinka Hakes Noble; illustrations copyright © 1980 by Steven Kellogg.

Dutton Children's Books, a division of Penguin Books USA Inc.: "Under the Ground" from *Stories To Begin On* by Rhoda W. Bacmeister. Text copyright 1940 by E. P. Dutton, renewed © 1968 by Rhoda W. Bacmeister. From *It's an Armadillo!* by Bianca Lavies. Copyright © 1989 by Bianca Lavies.

Four Winds Press, an imprint of Macmillan Publishing Company: *The Goat In the Rug* by Charles Blood and Martin Link, illustrated by Nancy Winslow Parker. Text copyright © 1980 by Charles Blood and Martin Link; illustrations copyright © 1980 by Nancy Winslow Parker.

Greenwillow Books, a division of William Morrow & Company, Inc.: "My Creature" from *Rainy Rainy Saturday* by Jack Prelutsky, illustrated by Marylin Hafner. Text copyright © 1980 by Jack Prelutsky; illustration copyright © 1980 by Marylin Hafner.

Harcourt Brace & Company: From *A Chinese Zoo: Fables and Proverbs* (Retitled: "Animal Tales") by Demi. Copyright © 1987 by Demi. "Fireflies" from *Dragon Kites and Dragonflies* by Demi. Copyright © 1986 by Demi. Cover illustration by Julie Vivas from *Possum Magic* by Mem Fox. Illustration copyright © 1983 by Julie Vivas. From *A Dinosaur Named After Me* by Bernard Most. Copyright © 1991 by Bernard Most.

HarperCollins Publishers: Cover illustration by Carolyn Croll from *The Big Balloon Race* by Eleanor Coerr. Illustration copyright © 1981 by Carolyn Croll. From *Ant Cities* by Arthur Dorros. Copyright © 1978 by Arthur Dorros. From *Four & Twenty Dinosaurs* by Bernard Most. Copyright © 1990 by Bernard Most. *The Chalk Doll* by Charlotte Pomerantz, illustrated by Frané Lessac. Text copyright © 1989 by Charlotte Pomerantz; illustrations copyright © 1989 by Frané Lessac. "Instructions" from *Where the Sidewalk Ends* by Shel Silverstein. Copyright © 1974 by Evil Eye Music, Inc.

Heian International, Inc.: Cover illustration from *Wally, the Whale Who Loved Balloons* by Yuichi Watanabe. © 1982 by Yuichi Watanabe.

Holiday House, Inc.: Cover illustration from *The Great Trash Bash* by Loreen Leedy. Copyright © 1991 by Loreen Leedy.

Henry Holt and Company, Inc.: *The Empty Pot* by Demi. Copyright © 1990 by Demi. Cover illustration by Megan Lloyd from *Spoonbill Swamp* by Brenda Z. Guiberson. Illustration copyright © 1992 by Megan Lloyd.

Kane/Miller Book Publishers: *The Night of the Stars* by Douglas Gutiérrez and María Fernandez Oliver, translated by Carmen Diana Dearden. Originally published in Venezuela in Spanish under the title *La Noche de Las Estrellas* by Ediciones Ekaré-Banco del Libro, 1987. Published in America by Kane/Miller Book Publishers, 1988.

Harold Lavington and Jean Tibbles: "The Underworld" by Margaret Lavington.

Little, Brown and Company: Cover illustration by Carla Golembe from *Why The Sky Is Far Away*, retold by Mary-Joan Gerson. Illustration copyright © 1992 by Carla Golembe. *Awful Aardvark* by Mwalimu, illustrated by Adrienne Kennaway. Text copyright © 1989 by Peter Upton; illustrations copyright © 1989 by Adrienne Kennaway.

Gina Maccoby Literary Agency: "Ants" from *Yellow Butter Purple Jelly Red Jam Black Bread* by Mary Ann Hoberman. Text copyright © 1981 by Mary Ann Hoberman. Published by Viking Penguin.

North-South Books Inc., New York: Cover illustration by Agnès Mathieu from *Arthur Sets Sail* by Libor Schaffer. Copyright © 1987 by Nord-Süd Verlag AG. Originally published in Switzerland under the title *Erwin, das abenteuerlustige Erdferkel.*

continued on page 336

Dear Reader,

Wouldn't you like a dinosaur? How about a silly snake or a friendly whale? You don't have to look too far to find them. They are all waiting for you inside this book.

As you turn the pages, your adventure will begin. You'll go from Jamaica to Russia and to many places in between. You will paint pictures on a house with a boy in Panama, smell a "thunder cake" baking, and spend some time inside an anthill.

All Kinds of Friends will make you laugh, think, and learn. We invite you to join us as we travel around the world through stories.

Sincerely,

The Authors

Unit One
Unusual Zoo / 10

Unit Two
World Corners / 102

UNIT THREE
Side by Side / 208

8

UNIT ONE 1

Unusual Zoo

The animals in this unusual zoo come from near and far, from today and yesterday. Some are real and some are made up. Artists such as Maurice Sendak use their imaginations to draw and write about unusual animals. What kinds of animals can you find in an unusual zoo? Turn the pages of this unit to find out.

THEMES

BOOKSHELF

SPOONBILL SWAMP

by Brenda Z. Guiberson

A mother spoonbill flies to the swamp to find food for her babies. A mother alligator swims in the swamp to find food for *her* babies. Find out what happens when the spoonbill meets the alligator.

Harcourt Brace Library Book

DEREK THE KNITTING DINOSAUR

by Mary Blackwood

Sometimes Derek feels bad that he isn't more like his brothers Fang and Fearless. He likes to knit—they like to roar! Derek knits and knits until his house is filled with sweaters, socks, and more. Then one day, Derek's knitting saves his brothers!

Harcourt Brace Library Book

FEATHERS LIKE A RAINBOW

by Flora

Long ago all the birds of the rain forest had dark feathers. "Why can't I have feathers as beautiful as the rainbow?" asks Jacamin. Find out what happens when Jacamin's mother tries to find colors for his feathers.

POSSUM MAGIC

by Mem Fox

Grandma Poss makes her granddaughter Hush invisible. Then Hush wants to see herself again. Join the two possums as they look all around for just the right food to make Hush reappear.

ARTHUR SETS SAIL

by Libor Schaffer

Arthur leaves the land of the aardvarks and sails across the ocean looking for adventure. He finds the land of the rosy-pink pigs. Can aardvarks and pigs get along?

THEME

Nighttime Animals

Some animals sleep at night, just as you do. Other animals sleep during the day and are awake at night. Read the following stories and poem to find out about two unusual nighttime animals, Aardvark and an armadillo.

CONTENTS

15

AWFUL AARDVARK

Mwalimu and
Adrienne Kennaway

NOTABLE
CHILDREN'S
TRADE BOOK IN
THE FIELD OF
SOCIAL STUDIES

Aardvark was asleep in his favorite tree. The tree was old and dry, but it had a smooth branch where Aardvark would lie and rest his long nose.

And what a nose! His snoring was so loud that it kept Mongoose and all the other animals awake night after night. HHHRRR—ZZZZ! went Aardvark's nose.

"How awful," Mongoose yawned. "I wish he would keep quiet or go somewhere else."

Aardvark only stopped snoring when the sun came up. Then he clambered to the ground and set off to hunt for tasty grubs and crunchy beetles.

While Aardvark was hunting for breakfast, Mongoose had an idea. "I will just have to annoy him more than he annoys me," he decided.

First Mongoose had a meeting with the Monkeys.

Next he went to
see Lion.

Then he talked to
Rhinoceros.

19

That night, as usual, Aardvark climbed up to his branch in the tree and very soon he was snoring HHHRRR—ZZZZ!

Mongoose called into the darkness. The Monkeys came, and the tree shook as they chattered and screeched in the branches.

Aardvark woke up. "Stop making that noise," he shouted. But he soon went back to sleep and snored even more loudly than before. HHHRRR—ZZZZ!

Then Mongoose called out again. There was a low, rumbling growl as Lion came pad-pad-padding to the tree where Aardvark was snoring.

Stretching his legs and reaching high, Lion SCRAAATCHED the bark with his strong claws.

Aardvark woke up again. "Stop it! Go away!" he shouted. But soon he was snoring again, louder than ever. HHHRRR—ZZZZ!

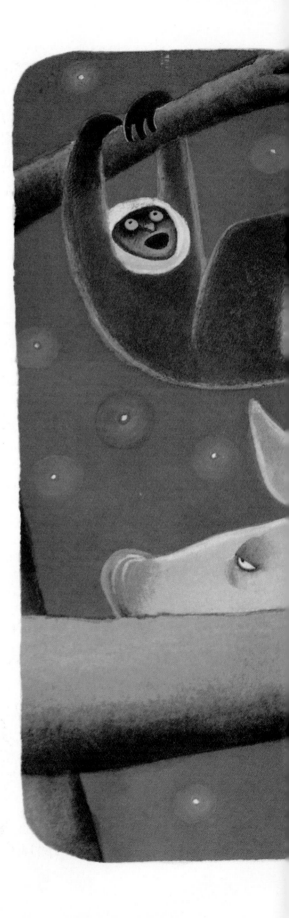

Now Mongoose was very angry. He was so angry that his fur bristled. He sent out another call. The ground trembled as Rhinoceros came puff-puff-puffing to the tree. BUMP! Aardvark nearly fell off the branch when Rhinoceros pushed his fat bottom against the trunk.

"Go away! Leave me alone!" cried Aardvark. But still he did not stay awake for long. HHHRRR—ZZZZ!

"We need help," puffed Rhinoceros. "I'll tell you what we'll do."

Soon there came a munch-munch-munching sound from the roots of the tree.

Aardvark just kept on snoring.

Suddenly there was a loud snap and a crack. SNAP! went the roots. CRAAAAACK went the tree and it toppled over.

Aardvark bounced to the ground.

He picked himself up and glared at the other animals. "Who did that? Who pushed my tree over?" he demanded.

"Not me," said Lion.

"Not me," said Rhinoceros.

"Not us," said the Monkeys.

Aardvark snorted at Mongoose. "It was you."

"Not me," said Mongoose. "They did it." And
he pointed at the broken roots.

Aardvark saw that the roots of the tree had been eaten away by hundreds of termites.

"I'm going to gobble you up," he threatened. He stuck out his long tongue and ate some of the termites. Yum-yum. He licked his lips. "I think I'll eat you all."

The termites hurried away with Aardvark following and eating as many as he could reach with his tongue.

In the morning the termites hid in the castles of sand and mud which they had built to protect themselves. But at night they still came out to eat the trees.

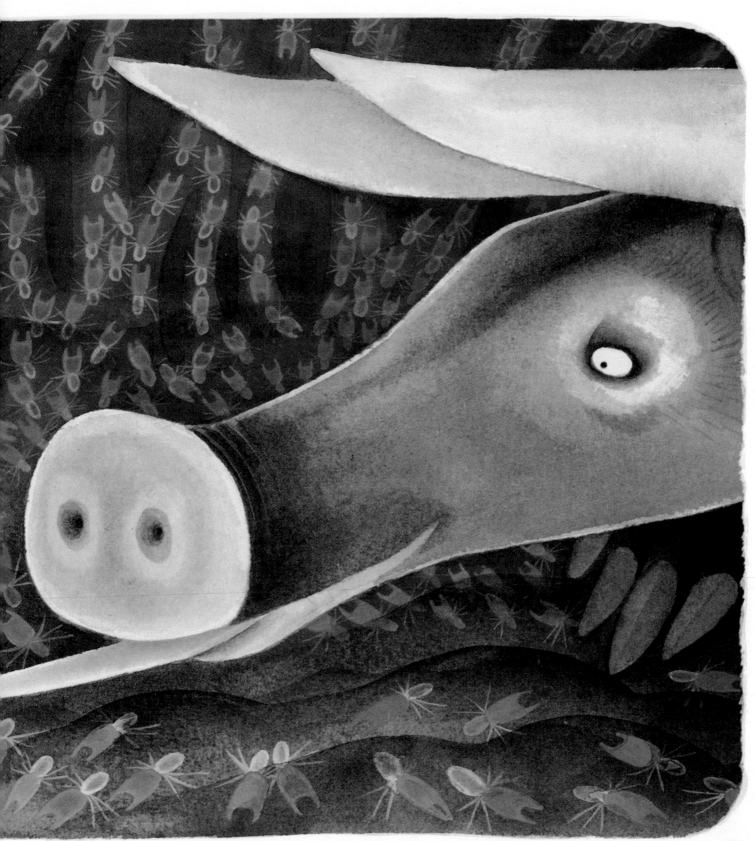

27

And from that time to this, Aardvark has slept during the day and eaten termites at night.

And Mongoose and the other animals sleep peacefully because they are no longer disturbed by Aardvark's awful snoring.

🌳 How would you have solved the problem of Aardvark's awful snoring?

🌳 Why does Mongoose decide to stop Aardvark's snoring?

🌳 Why does Aardvark stay awake at night now?

WRITE Imagine that you are Aardvark. Write a note to one of the animals in the story. Tell why you like to stay awake at night.

It's an Armadillo!

text and photographs by

BIANCA LAVIES

ALA NOTABLE BOOK

OUTSTANDING SCIENCE TRADE BOOK

What has left these tracks in the sand? Something with four feet and a tail. You can see its footprints. You can see the groove made by its tail. Where did it go?

It went into its burrow underground. The burrow keeps it cool in summer and warm in winter.

During the day, it sleeps there in a nest. In the evening, it will leave the burrow.

Here it comes. It's an armadillo!

There are several kinds of armadillos in the world. This one is called a nine-banded armadillo. The bands look like stripes around her middle. With her nose and claws, the armadillo roots up leaves and twigs. She is searching for food—beetles, grubs, and ant eggs. Sometimes she also eats berries or juicy roots.

Every now and then the armadillo sits up on her hind legs and listens. She cannot see very well, but she can hear the sounds around her: a leaf rustling, a twig breaking—even a camera clicking.

She also stops to sniff the air. Her keen sense of smell makes up for her poor eyesight. She can follow the trail of a cricket just by sniffing. Now she smells fire ants.

The armadillo starts to dig. Her long claws make her an expert digger. Then she sniffs the hole she has dug, searching for ant eggs. Ants walk along her nose. They try to bite her, but they cannot pierce her tough, leathery covering. This covering is called a carapace, and it protects her body like armor. *Armadillo* is a Spanish word meaning "little armored one." But the armadillo does have some soft spots—the skin on her belly, the skin between her bands, and the tip of her nose, for instance.

The armadillo's long, sticky tongue flicks in and out, in and out, lapping up the food she finds.

She has small, stubby teeth, but she doesn't use them for chewing or biting or much of anything.

Soon she ambles on, searching for more food.
She goes into dense, scrubby areas, where
her carapace lets her slip through tangles and
prickles. Her bands allow her to bend and
turn with ease.

After a while she wanders too close
to a road. Suddenly there is a flash of
headlights. What does the armadillo do?

She jumps!

That's what armadillos do when they are startled.
Then they run like crazy.

This armadillo is lucky. The car does not hit her.

She comes to a small river. To cross it she can hold
her breath, sink, and walk along the plants on the
bottom. Or she can gulp lots of air into her stomach,
float, and paddle along like a ball with feet.

Sometimes armadillos float on logs. People say they
may have crossed the big Mississippi River this way.
Nine-banded armadillos live in the southern United
States and all through Central and South America.

Now the armadillo looks very fat. Soon she
will have babies. To make her nest cozy for
them, she collects grass and leaves. She holds
the grass and leaves in a bundle between her
front and hind legs. Then she hops backwards.
As she hops, her tail guides her into the burrow.
She does this many times, until her nest is just
right.

In the nest, she gives birth to four baby armadillos, or pups. Each pup is exactly the same as the others. They are identical quadruplets.

Their mother's milk helps them grow. Armadillos are mammals. Mammals have hair or fur, and mammal mothers feed their young with milk from their own bodies.

The pups are lively right from birth. Their eyes are open, and they crawl all over their mother, and one another.

Their mother takes good care of them. She leaves her burrow less often now.

At first the pups' armor is soft, smooth, and shiny. It feels a little like wax. The armor will become tougher as the pups grow.

In a few months they will be big enough and strong enough to go out on their own. Until then they stay inside the burrow, drink their mother's milk, and play. They sniff one another and crawl all over each other until . . . they are all tired out. Then they snuggle up together and close their eyes.

They are ready for a good nap. Sleep tight.

🍁 What is the most interesting thing you learned about an armadillo?

🍁 How do you think the author, Bianca Lavies, feels about armadillos? Tell why you think as you do.

🍁 What else would you like to know about armadillos?

WRITE Imagine that you follow the armadillo one night and take pictures. Write about what the armadillo does and what time it does each thing. Draw pictures.

INSTRUCTIONS

If you should ever choose
To bathe an armadillo,
Use one bar of soap
And a whole lot of hope
And seventy-two pads of Brillo.

Shel Silverstein

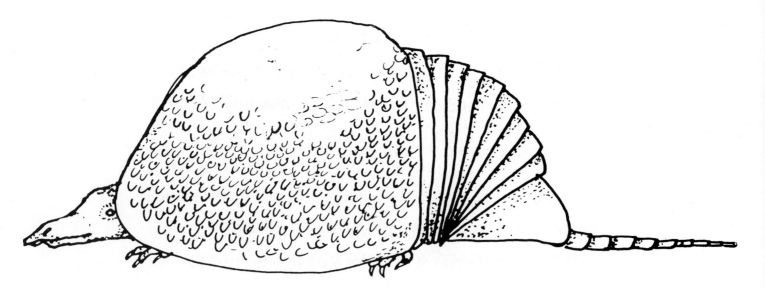

Nighttime Animals

How are the aardvark and the armadillo alike? How are they different?

If you took a picture of a real aardvark at night, what might the picture show?

WRITER'S WORKSHOP

How would you describe an armadillo to someone who has never heard of that animal? Write a paragraph that describes an armadillo. Use colorful words to help your classmates picture clearly what an armadillo looks like and how it would feel to touch it. Then you might want to put your work into a class book.

THEME

Silly Snakes

Have you ever seen a real snake? What was it like? Most people do not think snakes are funny. But in the following story and riddles, you will find that some snakes can be very silly!

CONTENTS

CHILDREN'S CHOICE
ALA NOTABLE BOOK

The Day Jimmy's Boa Ate the Wash

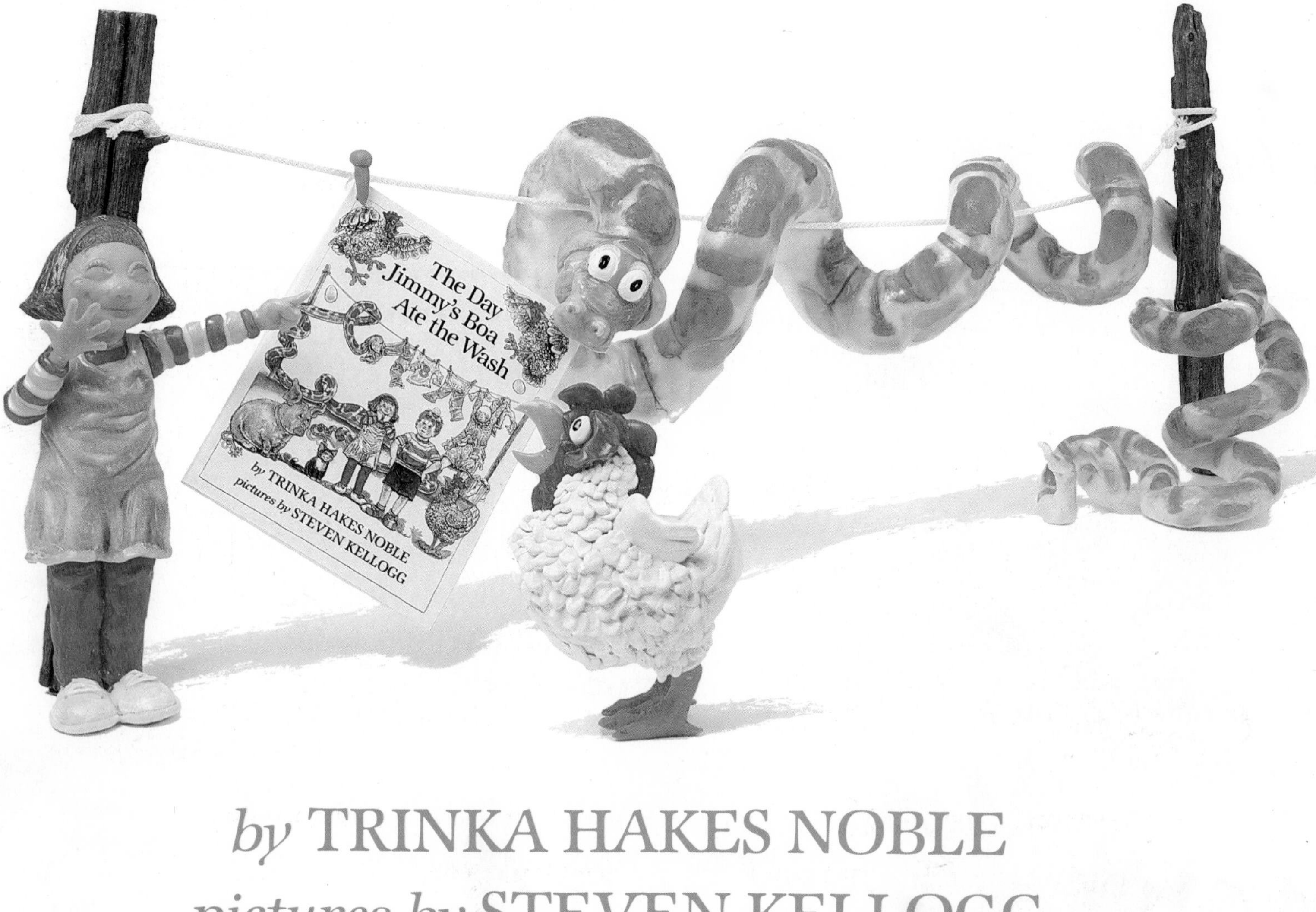

by TRINKA HAKES NOBLE
pictures by STEVEN KELLOGG

"How was your class trip
to the farm?"

"Oh . . . boring . . . kind of
dull . . . until the cow started
crying."

"A cow . . . crying?"
"Yeah, you see, a haystack
fell on her."

"But a haystack doesn't
just fall over."

"It does if a farmer crashes into it with his tractor."

"Oh, come on, a farmer wouldn't do that."

"He would if he were too busy yelling at the pigs to get off our school bus."

"What were the pigs doing on the bus?"
"Eating our lunches."

"Why were they eating your lunches?"

"Because we threw their corn at each other,
and they didn't have anything else to eat."

"Well, that makes sense, but why were you throwing corn?"

"Because we ran out of eggs."

"Out of eggs? Why were you throwing eggs?"

"Because of the boa constrictor."

"THE BOA CONSTRICTOR!"

"Yeah, Jimmy's pet boa constrictor."

"What was Jimmy's pet boa constrictor doing on the farm?"

"Oh, he brought it to meet all the farm animals, but the chickens didn't like it."

"You mean he took it into the henhouse?"

"Yeah, and the chickens started squawking and flying around."

HEN HOUSE SILENCE

54

"Go on, go on. What happened?"

55

"Well, one hen got excited and laid an egg, and it landed on Jenny's head."

"The hen?"

"No, the egg. And it broke—yucky—all over her hair."

"What did she do?"

"She got mad because she thought Tommy threw it, so she threw one at him."

"What did Tommy do?"

"Oh, he ducked and the egg hit Marianne in the face.

"So she threw one at Jenny but she missed and hit Jimmy, who dropped his boa constrictor."

"Oh, and I know, the next thing you knew, everyone was throwing eggs, right?"

"Right."

"And when you ran out of eggs, you threw the pigs' corn, right?"

"Right again."

"Well, what finally stopped it?"

"Well, we heard the farmer's wife screaming."

"Why was she screaming?"

"We never found out, because Mrs. Stanley made us get on the bus, and we sort of left in a hurry without the boa constrictor."

"I bet Jimmy was sad because he left his pet boa constrictor."

"Oh, not really. We left in such a hurry that one of the pigs didn't get off the bus, so now he's got a pet pig."

"Boy, that sure sounds like an exciting trip."

"Yeah, I suppose, if you're the kind of kid who likes class trips to the farm."

🏚 What is your favorite part of the story?

🏚 What starts all the trouble at the farm?

🏚 What things happen after Jimmy brings his boa into the henhouse?

🏚 What do you think will happen to Jimmy's boa?

WRITE   What will happen now that Jimmy has a pet pig? Write more to add to the story. Tell about the funny things that happen.

WORDS FROM THE ILLUSTRATOR:

STEVEN KELLOGG

When I illustrate a story written by another author, like *The Day Jimmy's Boa Ate the Wash*, I pretend I'm seeing the words in my head like the pictures in a movie. I try to think up pictures that will tell different things from the words. Sometimes the author lets me have some input into the story. For instance, *The Day Jimmy's Boa Ate the Wash* was originally called *Our Class Trip to the Farm.* After I drew the boa eating the laundry on the clothesline, I thought, "Hey, that would be a good title for the book." Happily, the author, Trinka Hakes Noble, agreed.

61

SNAKEY RIDDLES

What kind of shoes do reptiles wear?

Snakers!

What kind of slippers do snakes wear?

Water moccasins!

SNAKEY RIDDLES
BY KATY HALL AND LISA EISENBERG
PICTURES BY SIMMS TABACK

Silly Snakes

Which part of the story or which riddle do you think is the funniest? Why?

Make up a riddle about Jimmy's boa. Tell it to a classmate.

WRITER'S WORKSHOP

Imagine that you are Jimmy. Write a letter to a classmate. Tell how you ended up with a pet pig in place of the pet boa you used to have. Then you could deliver your letter.

T H E M E

Dinosaurs!

Do you like dinosaurs? In the next selections, you will read about many kinds of dinosaurs and about Bernard Most, who writes books about dinosaurs. You will also read about a dinosaur you might not want to meet.

C O N T E N T S

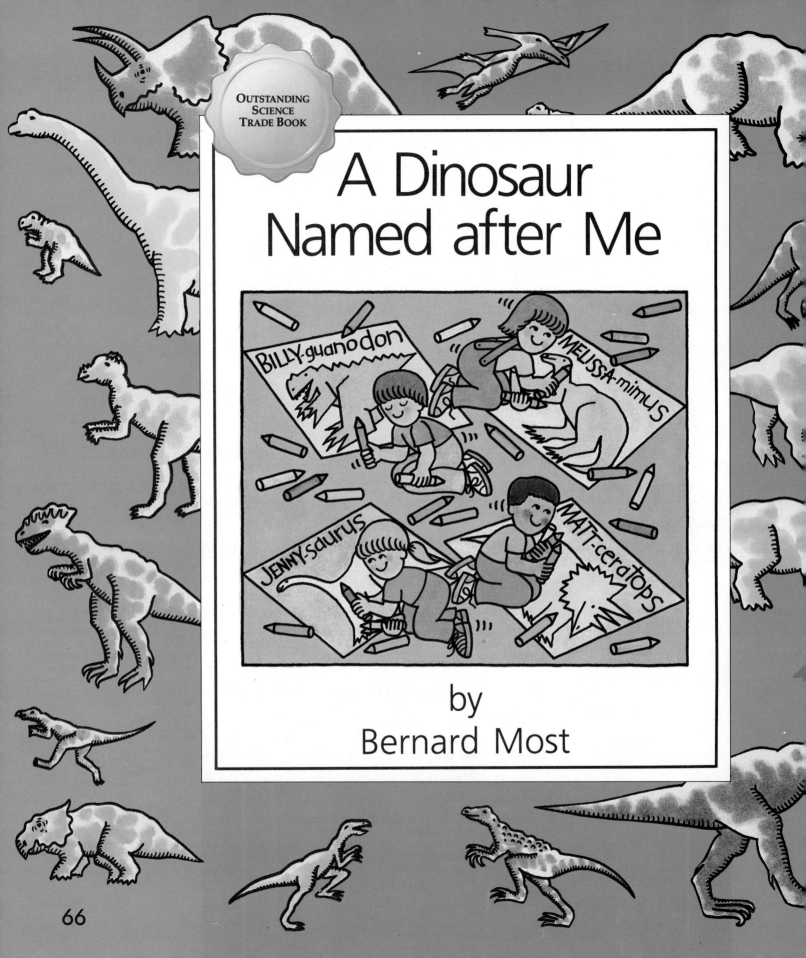

A Dinosaur Named after Me

by
Bernard Most

My favorite dinosaur was Triceratops . . . until
I read about Pentaceratops. Its name means
"five-horned face" because it had two more
horns than Triceratops. It also had a much larger
frill. Since I was born on the fifth day of the
fifth month, five is my lucky number. This
dinosaur should be named BEN-taceratops!

Ben

67

Apatosaurus (ah-PAT-a-saw-russ)

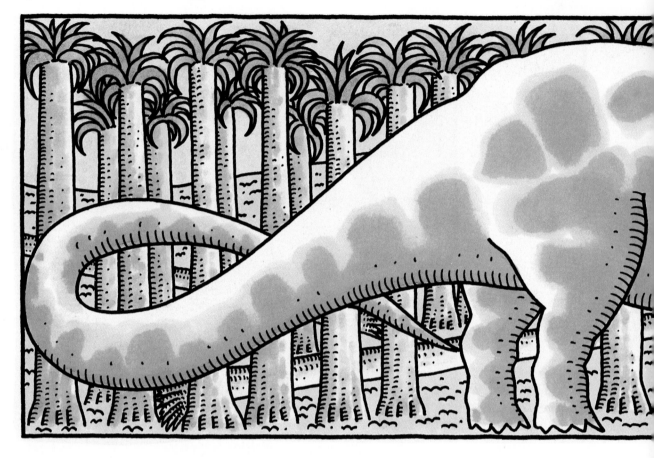

My favorite dinosaur is Apatosaurus. This is the correct scientific name for Brontosaurus, which was thought to be a new dinosaur when it was discovered. But scientists now think it is the same as a dinosaur discovered years earlier, Apatosaurus. I like the name A-PAT-osaurus much better anyway.

Pat

68

Ron

My favorite dinosaur is Brontosaurus. Everyone knows this dinosaur as Brontosaurus—so why change it? Many scientists today think dinosaurs were more like mammals and birds than reptiles. But no one wants to change the name *dinosaur,* which means "terrible lizard." If you must change the name of Brontosaurus, call it RON-tosaurus!

Brachiosaurus (BRAK-ee-a-saw-russ)

My favorite dinosaur is Brachiosaurus. It was a member of the tallest dinosaur family and could reach higher than any other dinosaur. I am the tallest person in my class, and I can reach higher than anybody. I would have named Brachiosaurus after me: ZACH-iosaurus.

Zach

70

Ankylosaurus (an-KILE-a-saw-russ)

My favorite dinosaur is Ankylosaurus. Rows of bony plates and a clublike tail protected this peaceful plant eater from meat eaters. Every time I visit the museum and see a knight's armor, I think about this largest armored dinosaur. But a much better name would be HANK-ylosaurus!

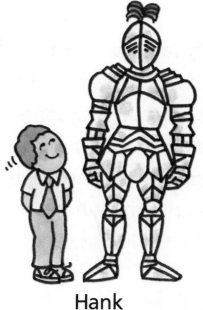

Hank

Microvenator (mike-row-ven-AY-tor)

My favorite dinosaur is Microvenator, or "small hunter." This turkey-sized meat eater was good at catching its dinner because it was very fast and had grasping claws. I'm a small hunter, too. I'm good at catching my friends when we play hide-and-seek. "Ready or not, here comes MIKE-rovenator!"

Mike

My favorite dinosaur is Maiasaura. Named "good mother lizard" because it was found near a nest with fifteen baby dinosaurs, scientists think it brought food to its babies and took good care of them. Mom says I take good care of my baby brother. She says this dinosaur's name should be MARY-asaura.

Mary

Stegosaurus (STEG-a-saw-russ)

My favorite dinosaur is Stegosaurus. Scientists think the large plates that covered its back were for protection and made Stegosaurus look larger to meat-eating dinosaurs—just like my shoulder pads protect me and make me look larger to opposing teams. My friends renamed Stegosaurus GREG-osaurus.

Greg

Dravidosaurus (dra-VID-a-saw-russ)

My favorite dinosaur is Dravidosaurus. It was a member of the Stegosaurus family but one of the littlest, only ten feet long. It's like a little brother to Stegosaurus. I'm Greg's little brother, so if they change Stegosaurus to GREG-osaurus, I hope they change Dravidosaurus to DAVID-osaurus!

David

Dinosaurs
(DIE-na-sawrs)

Diane

I don't have a favorite dinosaur, because they are all my favorites. I love reading about every one of them. If I had my way, I would change their name from dinosaurs to DIANE-osaurs.

Think about your favorite dinosaur. Wouldn't you like a dinosaur named after YOU?

 Which dinosaur is your favorite? Why?

 How did some dinosaurs protect themselves from enemies?

 How were all the dinosaurs alike?

WRITE　　You just saw a dinosaur! What kind was it? Write a story about it to read on a class news show.

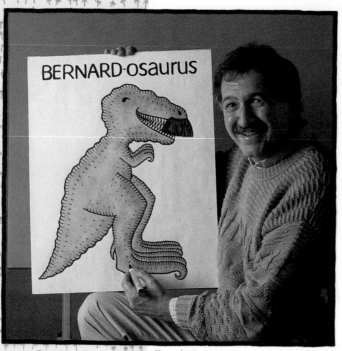

BERNARD·osaurus

Photo by Donato Leo

Words
from the
Author and Illustrator:

BERNARD MOST

I became interested in dinosaurs when my son Glen was in second grade. His teacher asked him to write down three wishes. One of his wishes was that the dinosaurs would come back to life. At the time, I was trying to come up with an idea for a picture book. When I heard Glen's wish, it was as if a light bulb went on over my head. I didn't know very much about dinosaurs, so I had to do a lot of research. I had to learn to draw dinosaurs so they looked like dinosaurs. My first tries weren't very good.

I got the idea for *A Dinosaur Named After Me* from autographing books. Sometimes people would say, "Make this out to Matthew-saurus." I decided to take some real dinosaur names and put them together with children's names.

When I'm not writing, I spend time with my tropical fish collection. I have a houseful of fish tanks. My other son, Eric, got me interested in fish. My other hobbies are music and making home videos.

The best thing about writing is seeing all the ideas and pages and pictures come together in an actual book. My favorite dinosaur is triceratops. I like to visit schools and draw a picture of a triceratops, and then underneath, I write READING IS TOPS!

Four & Twenty

Sing a song of sixpence,
A pocketful of rye;
Four and twenty dinosaurs,
Baked in a pie.

Dinosaurs

by Bernard Most

When the pie was opened,
They all began to sing;
Was that not a dainty dish,
To set before the king?

oland was a little dinosaur. He lived with his mother and father in a great swamp forest.

There were a lot of dinosaur children in Boland's neighborhood.

They played together every day, and Boland was friendly with all of them—all of them, except one. . . .

His name was Tyrone—
or Tyrone the Horrible,
as he was usually called.

He was just a kid
himself, but he was much
bigger and stronger than
most of the others.

He was a real bully
if you ever saw one. In fact,
he was the world's first
big bully!

Tyrone especially liked to
pick on Boland. He punched
and teased him and always stole
his snack or sandwich.

Boland tried to stay out of
Tyrone's way, but it seemed that
no matter where he went,
Tyrone was waiting for him.

Night after night, Boland had a hard time getting to sleep.
He kept thinking of ways to avoid Tyrone.
It seemed hopeless.

Boland's playmates tried to help.

"You have to get Tyrone to be your friend," Terry said to Boland one day.

"That's easier said than done," said Boland. "How do you make friends with someone who has been hurting and teasing you all your life?"

"You have to give him a present and show him you care," Terry said.

Boland thought for a while. What kind of present could he give Tyrone? Then he remembered how Tyrone was always taking his snacks and sandwiches. "A present for Tyrone?" he said. "Well, at least it's worth a try."

That afternoon, Boland went looking for Tyrone. "Here," he said in his friendliest voice. "It's such a hot day, I thought you might like a nice ice-cream cone."

Tyrone looked at Boland for a moment. Then he smiled a nasty smile. "Ice cream for me? How sweet!"

Tyrone grabbed the cone. Then he turned it upside down and squashed it on Boland's head.

"Ha ha ha!" Tyrone laughed and walked away.

Boland could hear Tyrone's laughter for a long time, echoing through the forest.

The next day, Boland told his friend Stella what had happened.

"You are taking this too seriously," Stella said. "Don't pay any attention to that big bully when he tries to tease you. Just stay cool. That's the only thing he'll understand."

"Staying cool when you are scared is not easy," Boland said. "But I will try."

And so the next time Boland met Tyrone, he stayed cool.

"Hi, Lizardhead!" roared Tyrone as Boland walked by. "How about MY sandwich?"

Boland did not pay any attention and didn't even try to run away. He kept on walking.

"I guess I'll have to help myself again," Tyrone said.
He stomped on Boland's tail until Boland let go of the
sandwich.

Boland tried not to show his tears. But it hurt a lot.

When Boland's friends found out what Tyrone had done, they were furious.

"It's time to fight back!" Stego said. "Tyrone has given you enough trouble. You must stand up to him and show him you are a dinosaur, too. You can win any fight against him. Tyrone just has a big mouth, that's all."

Boland was angry, too. "You're right!" he said. "Maybe I should fight him and stop this nonsense once and for all."

"Well," Stego said, "let's do it right now!"

The four friends marched off to find Tyrone.

Boland stood up and faced Tyrone the Horrible. "Listen, you brute," he said. "I have had enough of your bullying. Come on and fight!"

Tyrone took one look at Boland, then grinned and said, "Okay, if that's what you want."

It was a very short fight.

Little Boland had no chance against his big enemy.

"I'm sorry," Stego said. "That was not a very good idea. You'd better give up. Some bullies you just can't beat. You have to learn to live with them, whether you like it or not."

But Boland did not like it. "There just has to be a way to beat a bully," he thought.

He was still thinking as the moon came out and the stars filled the sky. Suddenly he smiled a big smile. "That's it!" he said to himself. Then he curled up and was soon fast asleep.

The next morning Boland took his sandwich and went off into the swamp forest as usual. It wasn't long before he ran into Tyrone.

"Another snack for me?" roared Tyrone. "I hope it's something good!" And with that he swiped the sandwich out of Boland's hand and swallowed it with one big gulp.

Boland walked on as fast as he could.

Suddenly he heard a terrible scream.

"AAaaaaaarghhhhhh!" It was Tyrone. Huge flames were coming out of his mouth. "HELP, I'm burning," he cried. "I'm dying! I'm poisoned! HELP, HEEEEEEELP!"

"Nonsense!" Boland said with a laugh. "It was only a sandwich. I didn't know you were so sensitive. I happen to like <u>double</u>-<u>thick</u>-<u>red</u>-<u>hot</u>-<u>pepper</u>-<u>sandwiches</u>. Too bad you don't." He turned around and went off, leaving the moaning and groaning Tyrone behind.

From then on, Tyrone stayed as far away from Boland as he could.

Boland played happily with his friends in the swamp forest all day, and he never had trouble falling asleep at night.

When much, much later some scientists found Tyrone the Horrible, he looked a little different—but he still had that nasty smile on his face.

🌙 What would you have done about Tyrone if you were Boland?

🌙 What is Boland's problem? How does he finally solve the problem?

🌙 Do you think Boland's friends give him good advice about how to solve the problem? Explain your answer.

🌙 Why do you think Tyrone acts as he does?

WRITE   Imagine that you are Boland or one of Boland's friends. Write a letter to Tyrone. Tell him how you and he can become good friends.

Dinosaurs!

What kind of dinosaur do you think Tyrone is? What kind do you think Boland is?

What do you think Bernard Most would write about Tyrone?

WRITER'S WORKSHOP

Imagine that you bring a very large, friendly, plant-eating dinosaur to your friend's birthday party. Write a funny story about what happens. You can make your story into a book to share with your classmates.

Multicultural Connection

A Wild Story

Maurice Sendak's father was a great storyteller. At night, he told his son Jewish tales that he had heard long ago in Poland.

These stories made Maurice decide to write books himself. He spent his free time writing and drawing pictures. When he grew up, he drew pictures for other writers' books. He wrote his own books, too. One of his best early books was *Where the Wild Things Are.* It won many prizes. Look at the picture that shows some wild things. Do you find them scary or funny—or both?

Draw your own picture of some unusual wild animals. Make up a story about them.

Science Connection

Night Animals

What do animals do when they stay awake at night? Where do they go? With a partner, pick an animal that you might see out at night. Find out facts about it. Then tell your classmates what you learned.

Music Connection

I Went to the Animal Fair

With a group of your classmates, put together a book of songs about unusual or funny animals. Draw a picture to go with each song. With your group, sing one of the songs for your classmates.

Unit Two 2

WORLD CORNERS

What is it like where you live? What do you eat? Maybe there is a special meal you and your family enjoy. In Japan, families have special foods for every season. You might enjoy the *shabu-shabu* they eat in winter. Read more about it and about cultures around the world in this unit.

THEMES

BOOKSHELF

THE ROOSTER WHO WENT TO HIS UNCLE'S WEDDING

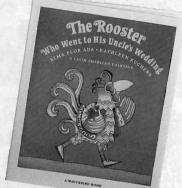

retold by Alma Flor Ada

A rooster needs help cleaning his muddy beak before he can go to his uncle's wedding. But the grass, the sheep, the dog, the stick, the fire, and the water won't help. Who finally helps the rooster?

Harcourt Brace Library Book

TWO OF EVERYTHING

by Lily Toy Hong

One day Mr. Haktak digs up an old brass pot from his garden. As his wife looks into the pot, one of her hairpins falls in. Out come two hairpins! What will the Haktaks do with this amazing old pot?

Harcourt Brace Library Book

FAMILY PICTURES

by Carmen Lomas Garza

Have you ever hit a piñata? Have you ever seen a Cakewalk? Find out about these things and more in this book about a real family.

ALA Notable Book, Outstanding Children's Trade Book in the Field of Social Studies

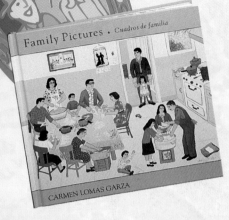

WHY THE SKY IS FAR AWAY

by Mary-Joan Gerson

Long ago the sky was close to the ground. People could grab a piece of sky to eat whenever they were hungry. Then something happened to make the sky go far away.

New York Times Best Illustrated Book of the Year

STOP THAT NOISE!

by Paul Geraghty

A tree mouse is trying to sleep. One by one, she asks the animals in the rain forest to stop their songs and sounds. Suddenly *all* the animals are quiet. What strange new sound do they hear?

THEME

Family Fun

Are there special things that you like to do with your family? Do you like to hear grown-ups tell about when they were little? In the next stories, you will read about the fun people can have at home with their families.

CONTENTS

The Chalk Doll

NOTABLE CHILDREN'S TRADE BOOK IN THE FIELD OF SOCIAL STUDIES

written by Charlotte Pomerantz

illustrated by Frané Lessac

Rose had a cold.
The doctor said to stay in bed
and try to nap during the day.
Rose's mother kissed her
and drew the curtains.
"You forgot to kiss me," said Rose.
"I did kiss you," said Mother.
"You didn't kiss me good night."
Mother went over and kissed her.
"Good night, Rosy," she said.
"I need my bear," said Rose.
"Your bear?" said Mother.
"You haven't slept with your bear
since you were little."
"I'm still little," said Rose.
She hugged her bear.
"Mommy," she said, "did you have
a bear when you were
a little girl in Jamaica?"
"No," said Mother. "But I had
a rag doll."

The Rag Doll

"I took a piece of material
and folded it over once.
With a pencil, I drew
the outline of the doll
on the material. Then I
cut along the outline and sewed
the two sides together.
Before I finished sewing
up the head, I stuffed the doll
with bits of rags."
"Did you like your rag doll, Mommy?"
"Yes, Rose, because I made it.
But I liked the dolls in
the shop windows more.
We called them chalk dolls."
"Did you ever have a chalk doll, Mommy?"

The Chalk Doll

"Yes, my aunt worked for a family
who gave her a chalk doll,
and my aunt gave it to me.
The doll was missing an arm,
and her nose was broken."
"Poor doll," said Rose.
"Oh, no," said Mother.
"To me she was the most perfect
doll in the world."
"That's because she belonged to you,"
said Rose.
Mother smiled.
"Now try and rest," she said.
"I'll bring you a glass of milk."
Mother brought the milk.
Rose drank half, then looked up.
"Did you like milk when you
were a little girl?"

Milk

"I loved milk," said Mother.
"But the milk was different.
It came in a can and it was sweeter and thicker.
Every morning, my mother took out two
tablespoons and dropped them into the tea.
We all got a taste. After breakfast,
Mother would cover the can with foil and hide it."
"Where did she hide it, Mommy?"
Mother shrugged.
"I never found out," she said. "But I watched her
every morning. And I dreamed that one day, when
I grew up, I was going to buy a whole can and
drink it all."
"Did you?" said Rose.
Mother was quiet.

"No," she said finally.
"I never thought about it till just now."
"Tell me another story," said Rose.
"I can't think of any," said Mother.
"Tell me the story of your birthday party."
Mother looked puzzled.

114

"My birthday party? We didn't have
birthday parties."
"What about the three pennies?" said Rose.
"Oh," said Mother. "That time."

The Birthday Party

"On the day I was seven years old, my
mother gave me three pennies.
I had never had so much money.
The pennies were cool
and smooth in my hand.
I went to a store and bought a little round
piece of sponge cake for a penny. Then I
went to another store and bought a
penny's worth of powdered sugar.
In the third store, I bought six
tiny candies for a penny.

When I got home, I sprinkled
powdered sugar on the top."
"I bet I know what happened then,"
said Rose. "Five friends came over. You cut
the cake into six little pieces and you had a
party. . . . But Mommy, you didn't
get any presents."
"No, I never did."
"Never, never?"
"Well," said Mother, "I did, if you count the
pink taffeta dress."

The Pink Taffeta Dress

"My mother was a seamstress.
She worked at home, sewing
for other people.
One year she brought home some
pink taffeta. Pink taffeta was my favorite.
She said she would try
and make me a dress for my birthday.
But she was so busy
sewing dresses for other people
that weeks and weeks went by
and she still hadn't touched the pink taffeta.
The night before my birthday,
I went to bed hoping she would
make the dress while I was asleep.
But when I woke up,
the pink taffeta material was still there.
I went to the yard and cried."

Rose leaned over and hugged her mother.
"Poor Mommy," she said.
"Did she ever make the dress?"
"Yes," said Mother.
"She finished the dress a month after my birthday.
It was the most beautiful dress I ever had."

"What kind of shoes did you
wear with it, Mommy?"
"No shoes, Rose.
We only wore shoes to church on Sunday."
"You mean you went to school barefoot?"
"Yes," said Mother. "Nobody
wore shoes except the teacher. . . .
But I *did* wear high heels."

High Heels

"The road to and from school
was paved with tar, and
there were mango trees on both sides.
We ate the sweet fruit and dropped the pits.
They dried in the sun.
We took the dried pits and rubbed
them into the tar on the road.
The tar was soft and sticky.

After we rubbed the mango pits
in the tar, we pressed the sticky pits
against the heels of our feet until they stuck.
Then we walked home clickety click clacking
on our mango heels."
Rose smiled.
"Clickety click clack," she said.
"You had fun when you were
a little girl, didn't you, Mommy?"

"Yes, Rosy. I did."
"Do I have as much fun
as you did?" Rose asked.
"Mm," said Mother, "what do you think?"
"I think I have fun too," said Rose.
"But there is one thing
I'd like to have that you had."
Rose got out of bed and went to
the sewing basket in the hallway.
She took out a needle and thread,
a pair of scissors, and some
scraps of material.
"What are you doing?" said Mother.
"I'm getting everything ready."
"Ready for what, Rose?"

"Ready to make a rag doll."
"But Rose," said Mother,
"you have so many dolls."
"I know," said Rose.
"But they are all chalk dolls.
I've never had a rag doll."
Mother laughed.
"Poor Rosy," she said.
And together they made a rag doll.

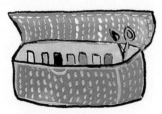

123

■ What do you think would be most fun about growing up in Jamaica as Rose's mother did?

■ What things did Rose's mother do as a child that you have also done?

■ Why did Rose's mother think that the broken chalk doll was perfect?

■ What did Rose find out about her mother from her stories?

WRITE Write about your own favorite birthday.

SO WILL I
by Charlotte Zolotow

My grandfather remembers long ago
the white Queen Anne's lace that grew wild.
He remembers the buttercups and goldenrod
from when he was a child.

He remembers long ago
the white snow falling falling.
He remembers the bluebird and thrush
at twilight
calling, calling.

He remembers long ago
the new moon in the summer sky.
He remembers the wind in the trees
and its long, rising sigh.
And so will I
so will I.

Catching Minnows-Town Meadows, Kent
by John Pedder (1850–1929)
Waterhouse and Dodd Gallery, London

THE

Little Painter

OF SABANA GRANDE

The Little Painter of
Sabana Grande

by Patricia Maloney Markun · illustrated by Robert Casilla

Award-Winning
Author

by Patricia Maloney Markun ◎ **illustrated by Robert Casilla**

High in the mountains of Panama lies the village of Sabana Grande. It is very small. Just seven houses of clay adobe stand alongside a brook in a grassy meadow. In the middle house lives the Espino family.

At dawn one cool purple morning, the rooster next door crowed. The Espinos woke up.

Papa went off to the meadow to milk the cow.

Mama stirred up the fire in the open-air kitchen and fried golden breakfast tortillas.

Fernando rolled up his straw sleeping mat and put it in the corner. He hurried to the kitchen to eat his tortilla right away.

This was an important day. At school Fernando had learned to draw colored pictures with crayons. Now school was out for dry-season vacation, and Fernando was going to paint for the first time.

His teacher, Señora Arias, had told him exactly how the country people of Panama made their paints. She said:

"Black from the charcoal of a burned tree stump.
Blue of certain berries that grow deep in the jungle.
Yellow from dried grasses in the meadow.
And red from the clay on the bottom of the brook."

It took him a long time to make the paints. Black was easy, because the burned stump of a big tree lay right next to the Espinos' adobe house.

But Fernando had to look and look before he found those certain berries deep in the jungle, to make the blue paint.

In the corner of the meadow he found a patch of very dry grass, and from that he made a large pot of yellow.

He wandered up and down alongside the brook, looking for clay. The fast-flowing water was too deep for him to reach down to the bottom. At last he came to a bend in the brook where the water was shallow. He reached down and dug up a fistful of clay. It was red, just the way Señora Arias had said.

Now his paints were stirred up and waiting—black, blue, yellow, and red, in four bowls. Next he got out the three paintbrushes his teacher had given him—one very small, one medium-sized, and one especially large.

I'm ready to paint pictures, Fernando said to himself. He picked up the small brush and dipped it into the pot of red. Then he had a terrible thought.

He had nothing to paint a picture on! An artist needs paper.

He looked in both rooms of the house. He could find no paper at all.

He ran from house to house asking everyone in Sabana Grande for paper to paint on. None of the neighbors had any. Not a scrap.

Fernando was sad. After all his work he wouldn't be able to paint pictures—the colored pictures he could almost see, he wanted to make them so badly. Paints and brushes weren't enough. He needed paper, too.

133

His fingers itched to draw something—anything. He put down the paintbrush and went over to the mud by the brook. He picked up a stick and drew in the wet dirt, the way he had ever since he was a very little boy.

The big rooster who woke him every morning came out of the chicken yard next door. Fernando looked at him and drew the shape of a rooster. He sighed. He couldn't use his new red and yellow paints to make a bright rooster. He couldn't make the rooster's comb red. He could only scratch out a mud-colored rooster. It wasn't the same as painting would be. It didn't have any color.

Fernando looked around at the adobe houses of his village. Suddenly he got an idea. Adobe was smooth and white—almost like paper. Why couldn't he paint on the outside of his family's adobe house?

"No!" Papa said. "Who ever saw pictures on the outside of a house?"

"No!" Mama agreed. "What would the neighbors say?"

Fernando looked at his pots of paint and was very unhappy. He wanted to paint pictures more than anything else he could think of.

At last Papa said, "I can't stand to see my boy so miserable. All right, Fernando. Go ahead and paint on the house!"

Mama said, "Do your best, Fernando. Remember, the neighbors will have to look at your pictures for a very long time."

First Fernando made a tiny plan of the pictures he was going to paint, painting it with his smallest brush on one corner of the house.

"Your plan looks good to me, Fernando," Papa said. "If you can paint pictures small, you should be able to paint them big."

Fernando picked up his bigger brushes and started to paint a huge picture of the most beautiful tree in Panama, the flowering poinciana, on the left side of the front door. As he painted, he could look up and see the red flowers of a poinciana tree, just beginning its dry season, blooming on the mountainside.

The neighbors were very surprised.

Señora Endara called out, "Come and see what Fernando is doing!"

Señor Remon said, "Who ever saw a house with pictures on the outside?"

Pepita, the little girl next door, asked, "Does your mother know you're painting on your house?"

Fernando nodded and smiled and kept on painting. Now and then he would look up at the mountain to see the real poinciana. After a week its flowers faded and died. Fernando's tree grew bigger and brighter and redder.

On one branch he added a black toucan with a flat, yellow bill. On another branch a lazy, brown sloth hung by its three toes.

The neighbors brought out chairs. While Fernando worked, they drank coffee and watched him paint.

Next he painted the wall on the other side of the door. An imaginary vine with flat, green leaves and huge, purple blossoms crept up the wall.

Word spread about the little painter of Sabana Grande. Even people from Santa Marta, the village around the mountain, hiked into town to watch him paint. The purple vine now reached almost to the thatched roof.

One day Señora Arias came from the school in Santa Marta. Why was his teacher looking for him, Fernando wondered. It was still dry season, when there wasn't any school. It hadn't rained for a month.

"School's not starting yet," his teacher said. "I came to see your painted adobe house that everyone in Santa Marta is talking about. Fernando, you did very well with those paintbrushes. I like it!"

She turned to the neighbors. "Don't you?"

"We certainly do!" the neighbors agreed.

They poured some coffee for the visiting teacher.

"Fernando, will you paint pictures on my house?"
asked Señora Alfaro.

"And mine, too?" asked Señor Remon.

Fernando nodded yes, but he kept on painting.

For fun he added a black, white-faced monkey
looking down at the people through purple flowers.

Next to the door he painted a big red-and-yellow
rooster, flopping its red comb as it crowed a loud "cock-
a-doodle-doo!"

Above the door he painted the words CASA
FAMILIA ESPINO, so people would know that this was
the home of the Espino family.

Now his pictures were finished. Fernando sat down with his teacher and the neighbors. Everyone said kind words about his paintings.

Fernando said nothing. He just smiled and thought to himself, There are still six adobe houses left to paint in Sabana Grande.

Would you like to be Fernando's neighbor in Sabana Grande? Why or why not?

How did Fernando change Sabana Grande? Tell whether or not you like what he did.

Fernando really wanted to paint, so he didn't give up. What else did you learn about Fernando?

WRITE Write about something *you* really want to do. Tell the steps you can take to make your wish come true.

Robert Casilla

Robert Casilla's favorite subject in school was art. "While other kids were outside playing baseball and football, I was at home drawing and painting pictures."

Robert Casilla especially enjoyed painting the pictures for "The Little Painter of Sabana Grande." This story takes place in Panama, which reminded him of Puerto Rico, where he lived for a short time as a child. "It was paradise to live in Puerto Rico. Painting these pictures gave me the chance to return there in my imagination."

"I love making pictures as my job, especially pictures for storybooks," says Mr. Casilla. "I hope that my pictures will help kids to learn and to enjoy reading."

This is what I looked like when I was your age!

Family Fun

If Rose could meet Fernando, do you think they would become friends? Explain your answer.

Rose's mother talks about the fun she had when she was a child. What do you think Fernando will tell his children about the fun he had as a child?

WRITER'S WORKSHOP

What are some good stories you've heard in your own family? Write a poem about some old family memories that you also want to remember. Use the poem "So Will I" to get ideas. You might want to put your poem into a class poetry newspaper.

THEME

A Lesson to Learn

Often you can learn a lesson from something you have done. In the next stories, you will read about a boy who learns a lesson and about animals who learn lessons. You can learn from these lessons, too.

CONTENTS

155

THE EMPTY POT

DEMI

A long time ago in China there was a boy named Ping who loved flowers. Anything he planted burst into bloom. Up came flowers, bushes, and even big fruit trees, as if by magic!

Everyone in the kingdom loved flowers too. They planted them everywhere, and the air smelled like perfume.

The Emperor loved birds and animals, but flowers most of all, and he tended his own garden every day.

But the Emperor was very old. He needed to choose a successor to the throne. Who would his successor be? And how would the Emperor choose? Because the Emperor loved flowers so much, he decided to let the flowers choose.

The next day a proclamation was issued: All the
children in the land were to come to the palace.
There they would be given special flower seeds by the
Emperor. "Whoever can show me their best in a year's
time," he said, "will succeed me to the throne."

This news created great excitement throughout the land! Children from all over the country swarmed to the palace to get their flower seeds.

All the parents wanted their children to be chosen Emperor, and all the children hoped they would be chosen too!

When Ping received his seed from the Emperor, he was the happiest child of all. He was sure he could grow the most beautiful flower.

Ping filled a flowerpot with rich soil. He planted the seed in it very carefully. He watered it every day.

He couldn't wait to see it sprout, grow, and blossom into a beautiful flower!

Day after day passed, but nothing grew in his pot.

Ping was very worried. He put new soil into a bigger pot. Then he transferred the seed into the rich black soil.

Another two months he waited. Still nothing happened. By and by the whole year passed.

Spring came, and all the children put on their best
clothes to greet the Emperor. They rushed to the
palace with their beautiful flowers, eagerly hoping to
be chosen.

Ping was ashamed of his empty pot. He thought the
other children would laugh at him because for once he
couldn't get a flower to grow.

His clever friend ran by, holding a great big plant. "Ping!" he said. "You're not really going to the Emperor with an empty pot, are you? Couldn't you grow a great big flower like mine?"

"I've grown lots of flowers better than yours," Ping said. "It's just this seed that won't grow."

Ping's father overheard this and said, "You did your best, and your best is good enough to present to the Emperor."

Holding the empty pot in his hands, Ping went straight away to the palace.

The Emperor was looking at the flowers slowly, one by one. How beautiful all the flowers were! But the Emperor was frowning and did not say a word. Finally he came to Ping.

Ping hung his head in shame, expecting to be punished. The Emperor asked him, "Why did you bring an empty pot?"

Ping started to cry and replied, "I planted the seed you gave me and I watered it every day, but it didn't sprout. I put it in a better pot with better soil, but still it didn't sprout! I tended it all year long, but nothing grew. So today I had to bring an empty pot without a flower. It was the best I could do."

When the Emperor heard these words, a smile
slowly spread over his face, and he put his arm around
Ping. Then he exclaimed to one and all, "I have found
him! I have found the one person worthy of being
Emperor!

"Where you got your seeds from, I do not know.
For the seeds I gave you had all been cooked. So it
was impossible for any of them to grow.

"I admire Ping's great courage to appear before me with the empty truth, and now I reward him with my entire kingdom and make him Emperor of all the land!"

How did you feel at the end of the story? Why?

Why do you think the Emperor gave the children seeds that would not grow instead of good seeds?

What lesson can be learned from this story?

WRITE   Write an ad the Emperor might place in the local newspaper to find someone to be the new Emperor.

Ms. Cooper, a writer, asked Demi some questions about her stories.

Cooper: Many of your stories take place in Asia. Is that a special place for you?

Demi: Oh yes. My husband, Tze-Si Huang, is from China, so that country is very special to me.

Cooper: Did you first become interested in China when you met your husband?

Demi: No. Many years before, even as a child, I was drawn to things of Asia. We had a Chinese rug in our house, a Ming vase with butterflies, and a carved Chinese chess set. All those things attracted me as a child.

Cooper: Where did you get the story of The Empty Pot?

 **Demi:** From my husband. One night, while he was cooking supper, he told me this tale. I rushed to get a pencil to write it down. The doorbell kept ringing, and he had to keep starting over, but eventually, I got it on paper.

Cooper: Was this a story he had heard as a boy?

 Demi: Yes. This isn't the first tale he's told me. I've used several of them in my books. They are stories that were passed down to him by his grandmother.

Animal Tales

ADAPTED AND
ILLUSTRATED BY

demi

FROM A CHINESE ZOO

FABLES AND
PROVERBS

白晝攫金

One day a big brown bear woke up and smelled some honey. Immediately he went outside and sniffed his way to a giant honeycomb, which was guarded by many bees.

He bit off a huge chunk of the comb and ran off with it in his mouth. The bees buzzed right after him, and each one stung him on the nose.

"You stupid bear," they said. "Why did you take the honey when all of us were right there watching you do it?"

"When I took the honey, I did not notice any of you," said the big brown bear. "I saw only the honey."

We frequently see only what we want to see.

When the tiger was out hunting one day deep in the forest, he caught a fox.

As he prepared to eat his prey, the fox said to the tiger, "You must not eat me. I am the king of the forest. Come with me and I will show you how the other animals fear me."

狐假虎威

174

When the other animals saw the big tiger following the fox, they scattered in many different directions.

"I see what you mean," said the tiger, not realizing it was from him, not the fox, that the animals were fleeing. "I'd better find something else to eat."

Small creatures must live by their wits.

Fireflies

from <u>DRAGON KITES AND DRAGONFLIES</u>
adapted and illustrated by Demi

Fireflies, fireflies,
Tiny lanterns in the sky,
You fly up high,
You fly down low;
Now on sister's
Dress you glow.

A Lesson to Learn

How are the Emperor in "The Empty Pot" and the fox in "Animal Tales" alike?

What lessons did you learn from the stories in this unit?

WRITER'S WORKSHOP

There are good lessons to learn in fables and folktales from all over the world. Read one of these tales, and write a book report about it. At the end, tell about the lesson that the story teaches. Then you could put your report and the book where others can read them.

THEME

Helping Hands

Can you think of a time when you made someone smile? Maybe you shared something special or gave help when it was needed. In the stories you will read next, the people who lend a helping hand make everyone else very happy.

CONTENTS

179

STONE SOUP

A Russian folktale by James Buechler
illustrated by Keith Baker

✳

CHARACTERS

Sergeant

Petya

Sasha

Olga, a seamstress

Dmitri, a carpenter

Anna, a baker

Marya

Villagers

Time: *Two hundred years ago.*

Setting: *A village street in old Russia. Nearby is a stream with stones in it. Dmitri, Olga, and Anna are hard at work in their houses. Three soldiers are walking down the street by the houses. One soldier carries a knapsack, and one carries a large kettle.*

Sergeant: Cheer up, Petya and Sasha! We've come through the forest safely. I'm sure the people of this village will share their dinner with us.

Sasha: I hope so. My stomach is empty. It feels like a cave.

Sergeant: I'll knock on this door.

Olga: Who is it?

Sergeant: It's only three loyal soldiers, tramping home across Russia. Can you spare us some food, good woman?

Olga: Food! No, I have nothing. Our harvest was bad.

181

Petya: I'll try knocking at this door. Hello in there!

Anna: What is it you want?

Petya: We'd like some supper, if you have any. We are three loyal soldiers tramping home across Russia.

Anna: I am sorry to see you so hungry, but you have come to the wrong place. It is everyone for himself in these times!

Sasha: Let us try this house. Maybe our luck will be better here.

Dmitri: Who is it? Sensible men are inside their houses, working.

Sasha: We are three soldiers, sir. It would be kind of you to share your dinner with us.

Dmitri: I have just enough dinner for myself. Go away!
(Dmitri shuts his door with a loud bang.)

Petya: What selfish people these are!

Sasha: They do not know how to share.

Sergeant: Let's teach these peasants a lesson! We'll teach them to make stone soup.

Sasha: Aha, stone soup!

Petya: That's just the thing.

(The sergeant, Sasha, and Petya huddle together to whisper about their plan. Dmitri comes out of his shop.)

Dmitri: Are you still here, you vagabonds? If you have no food, it's your problem. Why aren't you on your way?

Sergeant: Get some firewood, Sasha! Prepare the kettle, Petya. We will build our fire here, on this spot.

(Sasha gets some firewood. Petya gets two Y-shaped sticks on which to hang the kettle.)

Petya: We can use these sticks to hang the kettle, Sergeant.

Sergeant: Perfect, Petya. Now for the stones. Go and find some tasty stones in that stream over there.

Petya: I'm on my way, Sergeant.

(Petya runs to the nearby stream and selects some stones carefully. Dmitri, Olga, Anna, Marya and the other villagers come to see what the soldiers are doing.)

Dmitri: I do not understand. What did you say you are cooking here?

Sergeant: Oh, it's just some stone soup. Tell me, what kind of stone do you like yourself? You might help us choose.

Dmitri: I! Why, I never heard of making soup from stones!

Sasha: You've never heard of stone soup? I don't believe it.

(Petya returns from the stream with a bowl of stones.)

Sergeant: Come, sir. You must dine with us. Have you some good stones there, Petya? Let Sasha choose tonight.

(Sasha looks at each stone carefully and selects a chunky one.)

Sasha: Hm-m! This chunky one will be good! Ugh! Throw that flat stone away. A flat stone has a flat taste. Fill the kettle with water, Petya. My fire is ready.

(Petya fills the kettle with water. He then hangs it over the fire.)

Sergeant: Have you a spoon? We soldiers often make do with a stick. But for a guest, the soup will need proper stirring.

Dmitri: I have just the thing. It has a nice long handle. It is in perfect condition. I have not had guests in five years.

Sergeant: Splendid, you generous man!

(Dmitri goes to get the spoon from his house.)

Anna: What's this? The soldiers are making a soup from stones?

Marya: Yes! They are using stones from our own brook. That soldier put them in. I saw him myself.

Sasha: This soup smells so good. It's making me hungry!

Dmitri: Here's the spoon. Please be careful.

Sergeant: Sir, you shall be served first.

(The sergeant stirs the soup.)

Marya: I am more hungry than usual. It must be the smell of this soup they are cooking.

Anna: I must have a cold, for I can smell nothing.

Marya: Yes, I am very hungry, indeed. I have worked in the fields since morning.

Sergeant: Let's taste the soup now, Sasha and Petya.

(The soldiers each taste the soup.)

Villagers: Is it good?

Petya: It tastes very good.

Sasha: Oh, it tastes wonderful!

Sergeant: It might stand an onion, though. Onion is very good for pulling the flavor from a stone.

Olga: You know, I might find an onion in my house.

(Olga goes to get some onions.)

Sasha: It could stand a bit of carrot as well.

Anna: Perhaps I could fetch some carrots for this soup.

Sergeant: That is gracious of you. Will you bring a bowl for yourself, as well? You must dine with us.

(Anna goes to her house and returns with some carrots, a bowl, and a spoon. Olga returns with a bag of onions.)

189

Olga: Here are some onions. I should like to learn to make this soup.

Anna: Here are the carrots.

Petya: It could use just a bit of potato, too. I cannot say that stone soup is ever quite right without a potato or two.

Olga: That is true. A stone is nothing without a potato!

Marya: If you need some potatoes for that soup of yours, I have a sack in my cottage!

(Marya gets her sack of potatoes from her cottage.)

Marya: Here's a full sack of potatoes.

Petya: Many thanks. Please stay for dinner.

Sasha: These potatoes will really add to the flavor of the soup!

(Sasha dumps the sack of potatoes into the kettle.)

Sergeant: Stop, Sasha. Stop!

Olga: What is the matter, Sergeant?

Sergeant: Sasha has added too many potatoes! The potatoes have absorbed the flavor of the stones.

Villagers: Oh, too bad! What a shame!

Marya: Is there nothing we can do?

Petya: I have an idea. Meat and potatoes go well together. Let's add some meat.

Dmitri: I have a ham. Wait here while I get it.

Sergeant: It might work, at that.

Dmitri: Here's the ham!

Villagers: Good for you, Dmitri! Quick thinking!

Petya: Thank you, Dmitri. I'll put it in myself.

Marya: Can anyone make this stone soup?

Petya: Oh, yes. All you need are stones, fire, water, and hungry people.

Anna: Well, how is it now, soldier? It smells delicious.

Sergeant: Friends, I know this will be a very good soup. You have fine stones in this village, no doubt of that! Stay and eat with us, one and all.

(The villagers get bowls and spoons. The sergeant fills everyone's bowl with soup. Then they begin to eat.)

Dmitri: This is truly a delicious soup, soldiers!

Anna: It has such a hearty flavor!

Marya: It fills you up!

Villagers: This soup is the best we've ever tasted!

Anna: And to think, neighbors, it's made only of stones!

Soldiers: Yes, imagine that! It's made only of stones!

The End

What was your favorite part of the play? Why?

What makes the villagers change their minds about sharing with the soldiers?

Tell about another way the soldiers could make the villagers share their food.

WRITE Write your own recipe for stone soup. Tell how you will get what you need and how to make the soup.

THE NIGHT OF THE STARS

Douglas Gutiérrez
María Fernandez Oliver

translated by Carmen Diana Dearden

Long, long ago, in a town
that was neither near nor far,
there lived a man

who did not like the night.

During the day, in the sunlight, he worked weaving baskets, watching over his animals and watering his vegetables.

Often he would sing. But as soon as the sun set behind the mountain, this man who did not like the night would become sad, for his world suddenly turned gray, dark and black.

"Night again! Horrible night!" he would cry out.

He would then pick up his baskets, light his lamp and shut himself up in his house.

Sometimes he would look out the window, but there was

nothing to see in the
dark sky.
So he would put out
his lamp and
go to bed.

One day, at sunset, the man went to the mountain.
Night was beginning to cover the blue sky.

The man climbed to the highest peak and shouted:

"Please, night. Stop!"

And the night did stop for a moment.

"What is it?" she asked in a soft, deep voice.

"Night, I don't like you. When you come, the light goes
away and the colors disappear. Only the darkness remains."

"You're right," answered the night. "It is so."

"Tell me, where do you take the light?"
asked the man.

"It hides behind me, and I cannot do anything about it,"
replied the night. "I'm very sorry."

The night finished stretching and covered the world
with darkness.

The man came down
from the mountain
and went
to bed.

But he could not sleep.

Nor during the next day could he work.
All he could think about was his
conversation with the night.

And in the afternoon, when the light began to
disappear again, he said to himself: "I know what to do."

Once more he went to the mountain.

The night was like an immense awning, covering
all things.

When at last he reached the highest point on the
mountain, the man stood on his tiptoes and, with
his finger, poked a hole in the black sky.

A pinprick of light flickered through the hole.

The man who did not like the night was delighted.

He poked holes all over the sky. Here, there,
everywhere, and all over the sky little points of light
appeared.

Amazed now at what he could do, the man made a fist
and punched it through the darkness.

A large hole opened up, and a huge, round light,
almost like a grapefruit, shone through.

All the escaping light cast a brilliant glow at
the base of the mountain and lit up everything below . . .

the fields, the street, the houses.
Everything.
That night, no one in the town slept.

And ever since then, the night is full of lights,
and people everywhere can stay up late . . .

looking at the moon
and the stars.

✳ Think about how the man solved the problem. How would you have solved the problem?

✳ How does the man feel about night at the beginning of the story? How does he feel at the end?

WRITE   Write an invitation for a "Night of the Stars" celebration. Tell why you are celebrating and what things you will do.

Helping Hands

Do you think that the soldiers have made stone soup before? Why do you think as you do?

Imagine that the soldiers come to the town in "The Night of the Stars" on the night the people first see the lights. What will the soldiers do?

WRITER'S WORKSHOP

What do you think the people in the town said when they first saw the moon and the stars? Write a short play about that night. Make up some characters. Tell what each one says about the new lights. Then you could work with a group to perform your play.

CONNECTIONS

Multicultural Connection

Food Festival

In Japan, every season has its special foods. In winter, families look forward to eating a special hot dish.

First, they pick up chicken meat with their chopsticks. Next, they swish it in a pot of boiling chicken soup. That swishing gives the dish its name — *shabu-shabu.* Finally, they dip the chicken in a spicy sauce.

Find out what foods people of other cultures have for special days or seasons. Then work with classmates to draw a mural of a food festival. Show people enjoying dishes from all parts of the world.

Health Connection

From Tacos to Tofu

With a group, plan a menu of healthful foods for a day. Include foods from many parts of the world. Draw a picture of a table set for each meal.

Social Studies Connection

A Taste of the Past

Tell about a culture your family is part of. On a map, point out the area where people from your family lived. Then describe a special family dish from that place.

UNIT THREE 3

Side by Side

When people work together, they can do wonderful things. Some African American women worked together to make old rags into quilts. The quilts are so beautiful that they hang in museums today. In the next unit, you will read about how people and animals work together to do all sorts of things. You might find an idea for making something with a friend.

THEMES

BOOKSHELF

HOW MANY STARS IN THE SKY?
by Lenny Hort

When a boy and his father can't fall asleep, they go out into the night to count the stars. How many stars do they see?

Harcourt Brace Library Book

THE GREAT TRASH BASH
by Loreen Leedy

Something is wrong in Beaston. Mayor Hippo looks around to find out what the problem is. He finds out that the town has too much trash! Find out how the animals of Beaston get together to "bash" the trash.

Harcourt Brace Library Book

Wally the Whale Who Loved Balloons

by Yuichi Watanabe

Wally the whale watches some people having a big party on the shore. He loves the balloons he sees. Find out how Wally ends up floating over the city!

The Woman Who Outshone the Sun

by Alejandro Cruz Martinez

Lucia comes to the village. Every day the river flows into her long, black hair. Every day she combs it out. One day Lucia leaves the village and the river goes with her. Why?

The Big Balloon Race

by Eleanor Coerr

Ariel falls asleep in her mother's hot-air balloon just before the big race! When Ariel wakes up, the balloon is high in the sky. Find out how Ariel bravely helps her mother.

Children's Choice

211

THEME

Working Hands

Have you ever made something special all by yourself? Perhaps you have received a gift that was made by hand. In the next selections, you will read about different things that were made by hand and how they were made.

CONTENTS

The Goat in the Rug

THE GOAT
IN THE RUG

As told to Charles L. Blood & Martin Link

BY GERALDINE

Illustrated by
Nancy Winslow Parker

by **Charles L. Blood & Martin Link**

illustrated by **Nancy Winslow Parker**

My name is Geraldine and I live near a place called Window Rock with my Navajo friend, Glenmae. It's called Window Rock because it has a big round hole in it that looks like a window open to the sky.

Glenmae is called Glenmae most of the time because it's easier to say than her Indian name: Glee 'Nasbah. In English that means something like female warrior, but she's really a Navajo weaver. I guess that's why, one day, she decided to weave me into a rug.

I remember it was a warm, sunny afternoon. Glenmae had spent most of the morning sharpening a large pair of scissors. I had no idea what she was going to use them for, but it didn't take me long to find out.

Before I knew what was happening, I was on the ground and Glenmae was clipping off my wool in great long strands. (It's called mohair, really.) It didn't hurt at all, but I admit I kicked up my heels some. I'm very ticklish for a goat.

I might have looked a little naked and
silly afterwards, but my, did I feel nice and
cool! So I decided to stick around and see
what would happen next.

The first thing Glenmae did was chop up roots from a yucca plant. The roots made a soapy, rich lather when she mixed them with water.

She washed my wool in the suds until it was clean and white.

After that, a little bit of me (you might say) was hung up in the sun to dry. When my wool was dry, Glenmae took out two large square combs with many teeth.

By combing my wool between these
carding combs, as they're called, she
removed any bits of twigs or burrs and
straightened out the fibers. She told me it
helped make a smoother yarn for spinning.

Then, Glenmae carefully started to spin my wool—one small bundle at a time—into yarn. I was beginning to find out it takes a long while to make a Navajo rug.

Again and again, Glenmae twisted and pulled, twisted and pulled the wool. Then she spun it around a long, thin stick she called a spindle. As she twisted and pulled and spun, the finer, stronger and smoother the yarn became.

A few days later, Glenmae and I went for a walk. She said we were going to find some special plants she would use to make dye.

rabbitbrush
wild onion
cliffrose
sumac
juniper
walnuts
dock

I didn't know what "dye" meant, but it sounded like a picnic to me. I do love to eat plants. That's what got me into trouble.

While Glenmae was out looking for more plants, I ate every one she had already collected in her bucket. Delicious!

The next day, Glenmae made me stay home while she walked miles to a store. She said the dye she could buy wasn't the same as the kind she makes from plants, but since I'd made such a pig of myself, it would have to do.

I was really worried that she would still be angry with me when she got back. She wasn't, though, and pretty soon she had three big potfuls of dye boiling over a fire.

Then I saw what Glenmae had meant by
dyeing. She dipped my white wool into one
pot . . . and it turned pink! She dipped it in
again. It turned a darker pink! By the time
she'd finished dipping it in and out and hung
it up to dry, it was a beautiful deep red.

After that, she dyed some of my wool brown, and some of it black. I couldn't help wondering if those plants I'd eaten would turn all of me the same colors.

While I was worrying about that, Glenmae started to make our rug. She took a ball of yarn and wrapped it around and around two poles. I lost count when she'd reached three hundred wraps. I guess I was too busy thinking about what it would be like to be the only red, white, black and brown goat at Window Rock.

It wasn't long before Glenmae had finished wrapping. Then she hung the poles with the yarn on a big wooden frame. It looked like a picture frame made of logs—she called it a "loom."

After a whole week of getting ready to weave, Glenmae started. She began weaving at the bottom of the loom. Then, one strand of yarn at a time, our rug started growing toward the top.

A few strands of black.
A few of brown.
A few of red.
In and out. Back and forth.
Until, in a few days, the pattern of our rug was clear to see.

Our rug grew very slowly. Just as every Navajo weaver before her had done for hundreds and hundreds of years, Glenmae formed a design that would never be duplicated.

Then, at last, the weaving was finished! But not until I'd checked it quite thoroughly in front . . .

. . . and in back, did I let Glenmae take our rug off the loom.

There was a lot of me in that rug. I wanted it to be perfect. And it was.

Since then, my wool has grown almost long enough for Glenmae and me to make another rug. I hope we do very soon. Because, you see, there aren't too many weavers like Glenmae left among the Navajos.

And there's only one goat like me,
Geraldine.

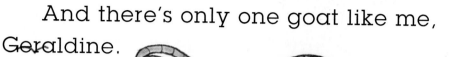

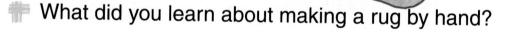

What did you learn about making a rug by hand?

What does Geraldine mean when she says,
"There was a lot of me in that rug"?

How do Geraldine and Glenmae feel about each
other? Tell why you think as you do.

WRITE   Do you have a favorite toy or piece of
clothing that was made by hand? Draw a picture
of something handmade that you have or would
like to have. Write about it.

ONE HAT, COMING UP!

THUNDER CAKE

by PATRICIA POLACCO

On sultry summer days at my grandma's farm in Michigan, the air gets damp and heavy. Stormclouds drift low over the fields. Birds fly close to the ground. The clouds glow for an instant with a sharp, crackling light, and then a roaring, low, tumbling sound of thunder makes the windows shudder in their panes. The sound used to scare me when I was little. I loved to go to Grandma's house (Babushka, as I used to call my grandma, had come from Russia years before), but I feared Michigan's summer storms. I feared the sound of thunder more than anything. I always hid under the bed when the storm moved near the farmhouse.

This is the story of how my grandma—my Babushka—helped me overcome my fear of thunderstorms.

Grandma looked at the horizon, drew a deep breath and said, "This is Thunder Cake baking weather, all right. Looks like a storm coming to me."

"Child, you come out from under that bed. It's only thunder you're hearing," my grandma said.

The air was hot, heavy and damp. A loud clap of thunder shook the house, rattled the windows and made me grab her close.

"Steady, child," she cooed. "Unless you let go of me, we won't be able to make a Thunder Cake today!"

"Thunder Cake?" I stammered as I hugged her even closer.

"Don't pay attention to that old thunder, except to see how close the storm is getting. When you see the lightning, start counting . . . real slow. When you hear the thunder, stop counting. That number is how many miles away the storm is. Understand?" she asked. "We need to know how far away the storm is, so we have time to make the cake and get it into the oven before the storm comes, or it won't be real Thunder Cake."

Her eyes surveyed the black clouds a way off in the distance. Then she strode into the kitchen. Her worn hands pulled a thick book from the shelf above the woodstove.

"Let's find that recipe, child," she crowed as she lovingly fingered the grease-stained pages to a creased spot.

"Here it is . . . Thunder Cake!"

She carefully penned the ingredients on a piece of notepaper. "Now let's gather all the things we'll need!" she exclaimed as she scurried toward the back door.

We were by the barn door when a huge bolt of
lightning flashed. I started counting, like Grandma told
me to, "1–2–3–4–5–6–7–8–9–10."

Then the thunder ROARED!

"Ten miles . . . it's ten miles away," Grandma said as
she looked at the sky. "About an hour away, I'd say. You'll
have to hurry, child. Gather them eggs careful-like," she
said.

Eggs from mean old Nellie Peck Hen. I was scared. I
knew she would try to peck me.

"I'm here, she won't hurt you. Just get them eggs,"
Grandma said softly.

The lightning flashed again. "1–2–3–4–5–6–7–8–9"
I counted. "Nine miles," Grandma reminded me.

Milk was next. Milk from old Kick Cow. As
Grandma milked her, Kick Cow turned and looked
mean, right at me. I was scared. She looked so big.

ZIP went the lightning. "1–2–3–4–5–6–7–8" I
counted.

BAROOOOOOOOM went the thunder.

"Eight miles, child," Grandma croaked. "Now we have
to get chocolate and sugar and flour from the dry shed."

I was scared as we walked down the path from the farmhouse through Tangleweed Woods to the dry shed. Suddenly the lightning slit the sky!

"1–2–3–4–5–6–7" I counted.

BOOOOOOM BA-BOOOOOOM, crashed the thunder. It scared me a lot, but I kept walking with Grandma.

Another jagged edge of lightning flashed as I crept
into the dry shed! "1–2–3–4–5–6" I counted.

CRACKLE, CRACKLE BOOOOOOOM,
KA-BOOOOOM, the thunder bellowed. It was dark and
I was scared.

"I'm here, child," Grandma said softly from the
doorway. "Hurry now, we haven't got much time. We've
got everything but the secret ingredient."

"Three overripe tomatoes and some strawberries," Grandma whispered as she squinted at the list.

I climbed up high on the trellis. The ground looked a long way down. I was scared.

"I'm here, child," she said. Her voice was steady and soft. "You won't fall."

I reached three luscious tomatoes while she picked strawberries. Lightning again! "1–2–3–4–5" I counted.

KA-BANG BOOOOOOOOAROOOOM, the thunder growled.

We hurried back to the house and the warm kitchen, and we measured the ingredients. I poured them into the mixing bowl while Grandma mixed. I churned butter for the frosting and melted chocolate. Finally, we poured the batter into the cake pans and put them into the oven together.

Lightning lit the kitchen! I only counted to three and the thunder RRRRUMBLED and CRASHED.

"Three miles away," Grandma said, "and the cake is in the oven. We made it! We'll have a real Thunder Cake!"

As we waited for the cake, Grandma looked out the window for a long time. "Why, you aren't afraid of thunder. You're too brave!" she said as she looked right at me.

"I'm not brave, Grandma," I said. "I was under the bed! Remember?"

"But you got out from under it," she answered, "and you got eggs from mean old Nellie Peck Hen, you got milk from old Kick Cow, you went through Tangleweed Woods to the dry shed, you climbed the trellis in the barnyard. From where I sit, only a very brave person could have done all them things!"

I thought and thought as the storm rumbled closer. She was right. I was brave!

"Brave people can't be afraid of a sound, child," she said as we spread out the tablecloth and set the table. When we were done, we hurried into the kitchen to take the cake out of the oven. After the cake had cooled, we frosted it.

Just then the lightning flashed, and this time it lit the whole sky.

Even before the last flash had faded, the thunder ROLLED, BOOOOOMED, CRASHED, and BBBBAAAAARRRRROOOOOOOOMMMMMMMM-MMED just above us. The storm was here!

"Perfect," Grandma cooed, "just perfect." She beamed as she added the last strawberry to the glistening chocolate frosting on top of our Thunder Cake.

As rain poured down on our roof, Grandma cut a wedge for each of us. She poured us steaming cups of tea from the samovar.

When the thunder ROARED above us so hard it shook the windows and rattled the dishes in the cupboards, we just smiled and ate our Thunder Cake.

From that time on, I never feared the voice of thunder again.

My Grandma's Thunder Cake

Cream together, one at a time
- 1 cup shortening
- 1 3/4 cup sugar
- 1 teaspoon vanilla
- 3 eggs, separated
  (Blend yolks in. Beat whites until they are stiff, then fold in.)

- 1 cup cold water
- 1/3 cup pureed tomatoes

Sift together
- 2 1/2 cups cake flour
- 1/2 cup dry cocoa
- 1 1/2 teaspoons baking soda
- 1 teaspoon salt

Mix dry mixture into creamy mixture. Bake in two greased and floured 8 1/2-inch round pans at 350° for 35 to 40 minutes. Frost with chocolate butter frosting. Top with strawberries.

What did you like about the story? What did you not like?

How does Grandma help the girl overcome her fear of thunderstorms?

Why does Grandma say the girl is brave?

WRITE   Think about something you helped make. Draw a picture of what you made, and write some sentences about it.

MY CREATURE

by Jack Prelutsky

illustrated by Tony West

I made a creature
out of clay,
just what it is
is hard to say.
Its neck is thin,
its legs are fat,
it's like a bear
and like a bat.
It's like a snake
and like a snail,
it has a little curly tail,
a shaggy mane,
a droopy beard,
its ears are long,
its smile is weird.

It has four horns,
one beady eye,
two floppy wings
(though it can't fly),
it only sits
upon my shelf—
just think, I made it
by myself!

picture by Marylin Hafner

AWARD-WINNING
POET

257

AN INTERVIEW WITH THE POET:
Jack Prelutsky

Ms. Cooper, a writer, asked Jack Prelutsky some questions about himself.

Cooper: Where did you get the idea for "My Creature"?

Prelutsky: When I was a kid, and the teacher said, "Draw a bird," everyone would draw a regular bird. But I'd say, "Hey, what if the bird had a horn?" So my creatures never looked like anyone else's. After a while I decided I liked my own creatures better.

Cooper: When did you start to write poetry?

Prelutsky: My writing came out of my drawing. I was trying to sell a book about imaginary creatures, so I had drawn lots of pictures to show the publisher. When I finished the drawings, I decided they needed poems to go along with them. The publisher didn't want my artwork, but she loved the poems.

Cooper: What do you do when you're not writing?

Prelutsky: I read a lot, I make funny little sculptures out of plastic, and I garden. I'm also inventing my own computer games.

AWARD-WINNING
POET

Working Hands

How do Geraldine the goat and the girl in "Thunder Cake" feel about the things they helped make?

How would Geraldine describe the rug that she helps make? Make the description rhyme like "My Creature," if you wish.

Writer's Workshop

Think of something you know how to make. Then write a how-to paragraph giving directions for making it. You may want to ask a friend to make it by using your instructions.

T H E M E

Insects at Work

Have you ever watched ants or other insects getting food? Did you know that ants live and work together in ant cities? In the following selections, you will learn more about ants and other insects.

ANTS LIVE HERE

Ants live here
by the curb stone,
    see?
They worry a lot
about giants like
    me.

Lilian Moore

UNDER THE GROUND

What is under the grass,
Way down in the ground,
Where everything is cool and wet
With darkness all around?

Little pink worms live there;
Ants and brown bugs creep
Softly round the stones and rocks
Where roots are pushing deep.

Do they hear us walking
On the grass above their heads;
Hear us running over
While they snuggle in their beds?

Rhoda W. Bacmeister

BUG POEMS

THE UNDERWORLD

When I am lying in the grass
I watch the ants and beetles pass;
And once I lay so very still
A mole beside me built a hill.

Margaret Lavington

ANTS

I like to watch the ants at work
When I am out at play.
I like to see them run about
And carry crumbs away.

And when I plug an anthill door
To keep them in their den,
I like to see them find a way
To get outside again.

Mary Ann Hoberman

Illustrations by Jennifer Hewitson

263

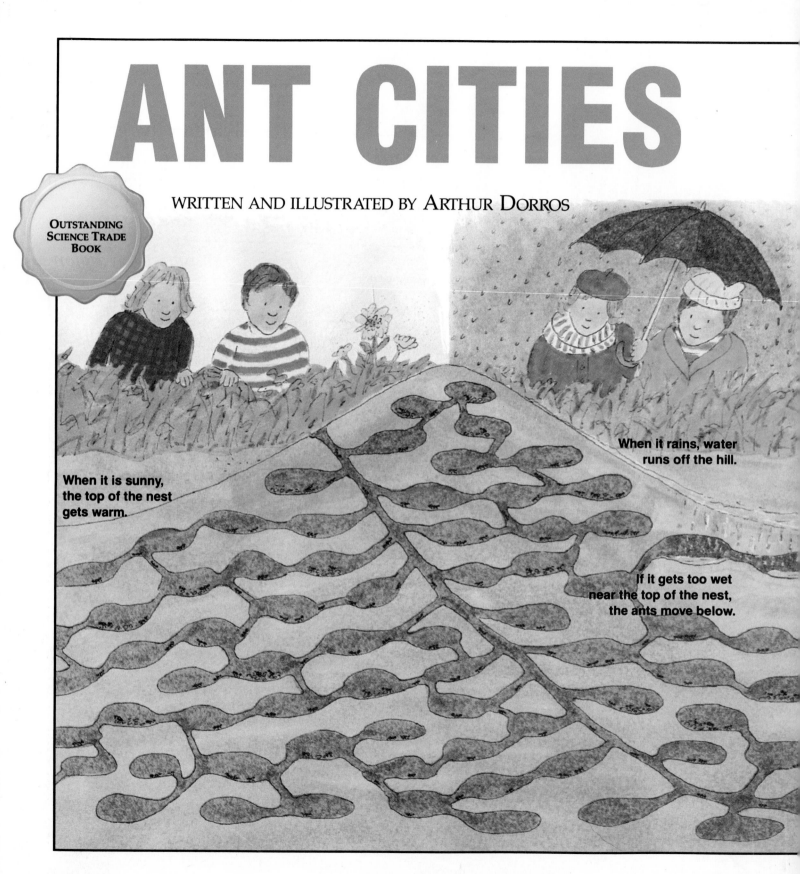

ANT CITIES

WRITTEN AND ILLUSTRATED BY ARTHUR DORROS

When it is sunny, the top of the nest gets warm.

When it rains, water runs off the hill.

If it gets too wet near the top of the nest, the ants move below.

In winter the ants hibernate in a deep room away from the cold. They stay together in a ball to keep warm.

Have you seen ants busy running over a hill of dirt? They may look like they are just running around. But the ants built that hill to live in, and each ant has work to do.

Some ants may disappear into a small hole in the hill. The hole is the door to their nest.

These are harvester ants. Their nest is made of lots of rooms and tunnels. These little insects made them all.

Underneath the hill there may be miles of tunnels and hundreds of rooms. The floors are worn smooth by thousands of ant feet. It is dark inside the nest. But the ants stay cozy.

In the rooms of the nest, worker ants do many different kinds of work. It is like a city, a busy city of ants.

Some ants have brought in food to the ant city. These harvester ants like seeds.

A worker ant cracks the husks off the seeds. Another worker will take the husks outside to throw away.

The ants chew the seeds to get the juices out. Then they feed the juices to the other ants.

Other workers store seeds for the ants to eat another time.

Not all ants store food. But harvester ants do.

In one room of the nest, a queen ant lays eggs. Workers carry the eggs away to other rooms to take care of them.

Each ant city has to have at least one queen. Without a queen there would be no ant city. All the other ants in the ant city grow from the eggs the queen lays.

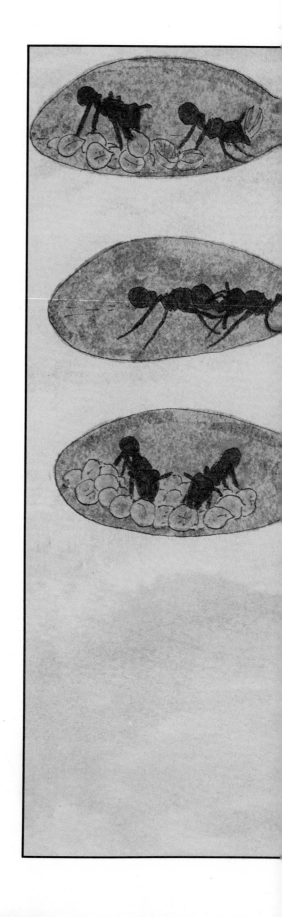

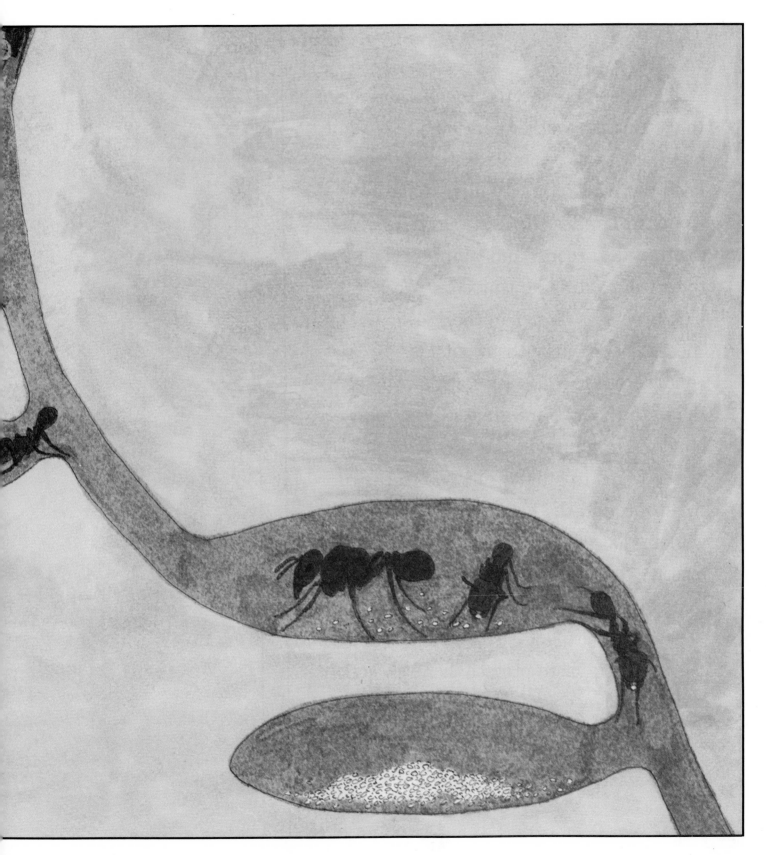

The queen doesn't tell the workers what to do. But the workers are busy. Each ant has work to do. Ants work together to keep the whole ant city alive.

Workers make the nest bigger by digging new rooms and tunnels. They use their feet to dig like tiny dogs. Workers pick up pieces of dirt in their jaws and "beards" and carry them outside.

Dirt from the digging is what makes the anthill. Ants are great diggers and builders. Imagine all the tiny pieces of dirt it takes to build a hill two feet high.

Out around the harvester anthill, workers look for food. Harvester ants mostly eat seeds. But sometimes they eat insects, too.

Ants can bite and sting other insects to capture them or to protect themselves. Be careful, because some kinds of ants can bite or sting you, too. Harvester ants will bite or sting if you disturb their nest.

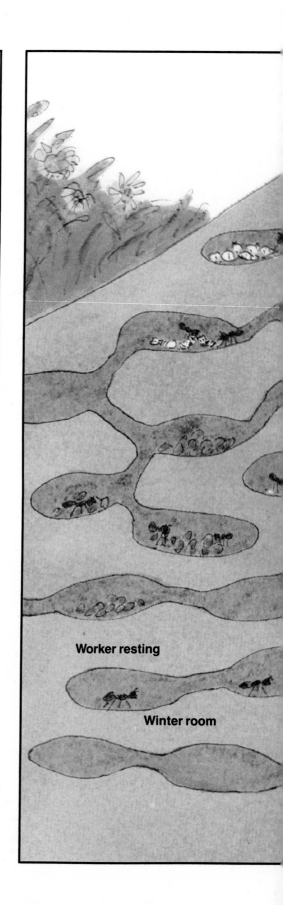

Worker resting

Winter room

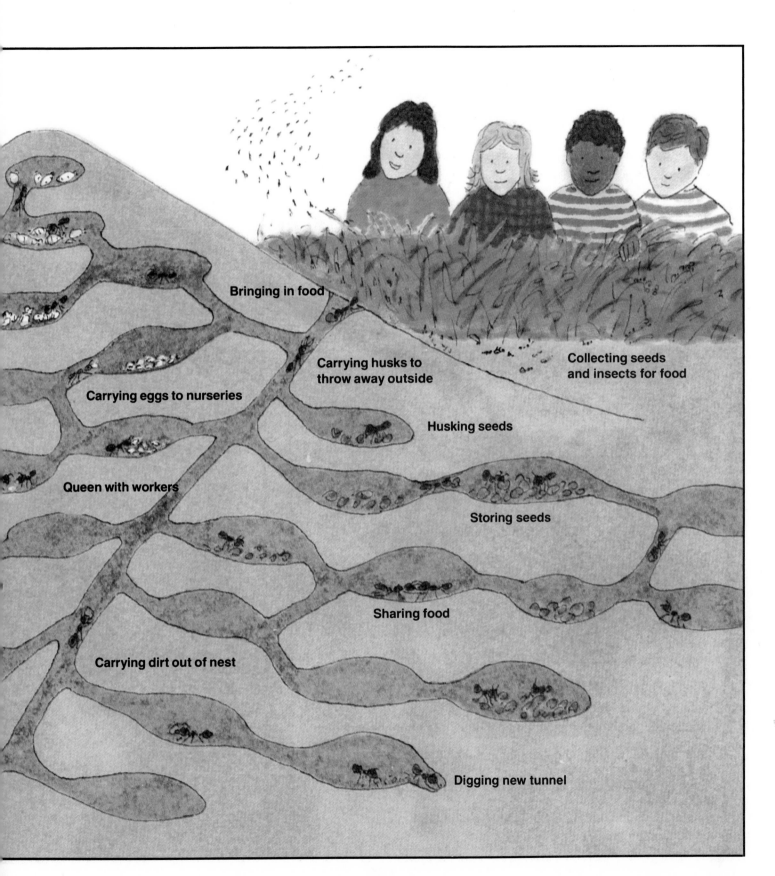

Bringing in food

Carrying husks to throw away outside

Collecting seeds and insects for food

Carrying eggs to nurseries

Husking seeds

Queen with workers

Storing seeds

Sharing food

Carrying dirt out of nest

Digging new tunnel

Ants use their antennas to help them find food. They touch and smell with their antennas.

Antennas

**Comb
on legs for
cleaning antennas**

If one ant finds food, others follow. Soon there will be a lot of ants carrying away lunch.

If one ant can't carry something, others may help. But each worker ant is strong. An ant can lift as much as fifty times its own weight. If people could lift like that, we could each lift a car.

The workers carry the food back to the ant city. Ants share the food they find.

Ants eat many foods.
But different kinds of ants
like different foods.
There are over 10,000
kinds of ants.

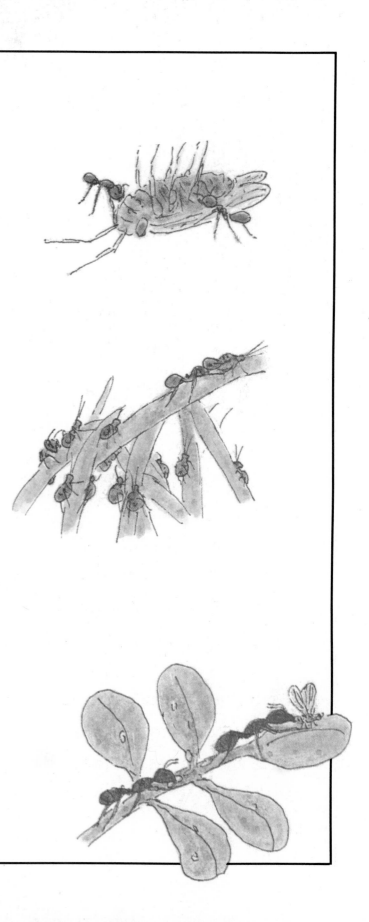

Formica ants mostly eat
juices that they suck from
insects they kill.

Cornfield ants like to eat
the sweet juices, or
"honeydew," they get
from aphids. Aphids
suck the juices from
plants. Then the ants
"milk" the aphids for
honeydew.

Carpenter ants especially
like sweet juices they can
get from insects, and from
plants, too.

Thief ants eat sweets and other food they find in people's houses and lying about.

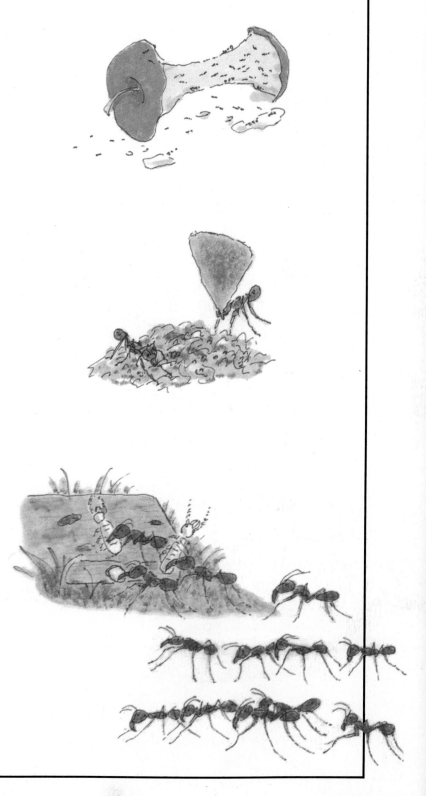

Leaf-cutting ants (parasol ants) make underground gardens with leaves they cut. They grow mushrooms in the gardens for food.

Army ants travel in large groups like armies. They devour huge numbers of insects, including termites.

The different kinds of ants have found many ways to make their cities, so they can live in many kinds of places.

Janitor ants make their nests in hollowed-out tree twigs. The soldier janitor ant—a kind of worker ant—has a big, plug-shaped head it can use for a door.

Many kinds of ants make hills or mounds. If you haven't seen harvester anthills, maybe you've seen the round-topped hills that formica ants make. Sometimes they cover their hills with thatch.

Formica ant

Pavement ants are tiny ants—1/8 inch long.
Harvester ants are about 1/4 inch long.
Some ants are as big as 2 inches long.

Or you may have seen pavement ants. They can live under the sidewalk.

Or carpenter ants, who build their nests in rotting wood.

There are small ant cities with just a few ants. There are big ant cities with many, many ants. Ants have been found at the tops of the highest buildings and on ships at sea.

Ants can make their cities almost anywhere. Look around and you'll probably find an ant city, busy with ants.

🌿 **What did you learn about ants that you didn't know before?**

🌿 **How is the ants' nest like a city?**

🌿 **If you were as strong as a worker ant, what would you be able to do?**

WRITE   What kind of ants might build a home in your neighborhood? Write the reasons for your choice.

Insects at Work

Do you think that ants always work and never play? What do you think a city of ants would do for fun?

Which underground creature is your favorite? Tell why.

WRITER'S WORKSHOP

Now find out more about your favorite underground creature. Write a report about it. You can use science books, magazines, and films to get information about your favorite ant, worm, mole, or other underground creature. Then you could share your report during a class nature show.

THEME

Earth Partners

Do you do things to keep the Earth clean and beautiful? Perhaps you recycle paper, bottles, and cans. Perhaps you care about saving animals. In the next stories, you will read about saving a hurt whale and a manatee named Sam.

CONTENTS

IBIS
A True Whale Story

by John Himmelman

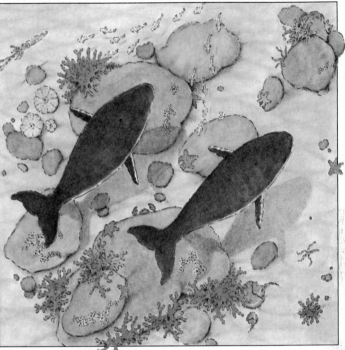

Deep in a bay, off the coast of an old fishing village, lived a pod of humpback whales.

One of the whales was a little calf named Ibis. Ibis was curious about everything in the ocean.

One day she and her friend Blizzard went out swimming. They saw many kinds of fish. The most interesting were the starfish. Ibis liked to look at them. There was something about their shape that made her feel good.

As Ibis and Blizzard were drifting over a reef they heard a strange humming noise. The two calves looked up to see something large and dark pass overhead. It was as big as a whale, but it wasn't a whale.

The calves were frightened. They had never seen a boat before. They swam back to their mothers.

The next day, Ibis went back to the reef. It wasn't long before another boat came along. Again, Ibis was scared. But she was curious, too. She forced herself to swim to the surface.

In the cool, hazy air, she saw several faces watching her. They didn't look scary. In fact, they looked very friendly. Ibis liked them.

In the months that followed, Ibis and her friends lost their fear of boats. Boats came in many sizes and shapes, and the people in them always seemed to enjoy seeing the little whales.

As Ibis grew up, she learned more about the sea. She knew what kinds of sharks to avoid, what food was the tastiest, and, best of all, where to find the most dazzling starfish. Ibis never got tired of looking at starfish.

People and their boats became a part of her life. Whenever a boat passed overhead, she swam to the top to say hello.

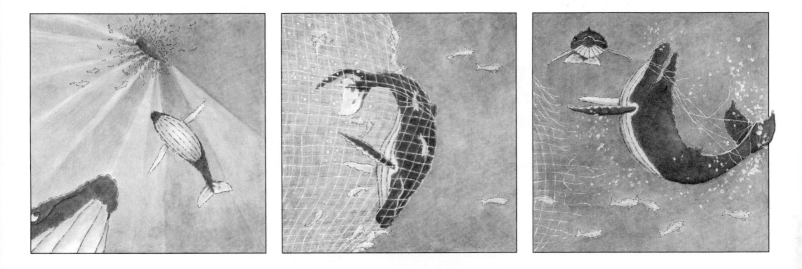

One evening, Ibis and Blizzard saw a school of fish swimming around the bottom of a ship.

Maybe there was something good up there to eat. They went to find out.

Suddenly Ibis was caught in a fishing net! She fought to get free. But the more she struggled, the more tangled up she became.

Finally she broke loose, but part of the net was caught in her mouth and wrapped around her tail.

Blizzard swam off to find help.

Ibis was confused and hurt. She wanted to get away, far from people and their boats and nets. Slowly and painfully she made her way toward the deep ocean.

Many weeks passed, and Ibis grew very ill. The net in her mouth made it hard for her to eat. And every time she went to the surface for air, the net cut into her tail. But if she didn't get air every half hour, she would die.

Winter was coming, and it was time for the whales to move to warmer waters. But Ibis felt too weak to make the long journey.

Instead she turned back toward the coast. It was so hard for her to swim, she could barely keep moving. Ibis was about to give up. Then she saw a familiar shape. It was Blizzard!

Blizzard saw that Ibis needed help. Gently Blizzard pushed her to the surface so she could breathe.

Suddenly the water was filled with the sounds of boat engines. The whales saw two small rafts and a boat circling them.

Blizzard and Ibis tried to get away fast. But Ibis wasn't quick enough. The boats rushed toward her before she could dive.

The people in the boats began to attach large floats to the pieces of net that were hurting Ibis. Blizzard stayed nearby, circling the boats nervously.

Because of the floats, Ibis could not dive. She began to panic, but she did not have the strength to fight. When the boats came in closer, a person reached into the water.

Ibis stared at the person's hand. The hand reminded her of something—something she loved very much. She began to feel better.

Soon many hands dipped into the water. Ibis felt them tugging at the lines of the net. Moments later the lines fell away, and she was free!

Ibis blew a big spout from her blowhole as if to say, "Thank you! Thank you!" Then she dived deep into the water. For the first time in many weeks, she felt no pain. She felt wonderful!

Blizzard joined her. Then the two whales popped back to the surface for one more look.

The people were waving their starfish-shaped hands.
Ibis knew the hands had helped her, and that the people
were still her friends.

Soon Blizzard and Ibis were leaping and diving with the other whales, far away in the warm waters where they would spend the winter together.

☆ How did you feel at the end of the story?

☆ Why does Ibis feel better when she sees the person's hand in the water?

☆ What do you think makes Ibis a special whale?

☆ What can you do to keep the area where you live safe for the animals that live there too?

WRITE Imagine that you were on the boat that rescued Ibis. Write a letter about Ibis to the captain of the fishing boat who threw the net.

Sam
the Sea Cow

Sam the Sea Cow

Francine Jacobs
Illustrations by Laura Kelly

CHILDREN'S CHOICE

READING RAINBOW BOOK

by Francine Jacobs *illustrations by* Laura Kelly

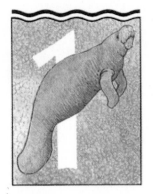

CHAPTER

Spring comes to southern Florida.
A huge, gray animal moves slowly
down a river toward the sea.
It is a shy, harmless manatee.

On her broad back, the manatee carries
a brand-new calf, just born.
He is three feet long
and weighs forty pounds.
His name will be Sam.

294

The manatee rises so her calf's head
is above the water.
Shoo-of! The calf breathes in.

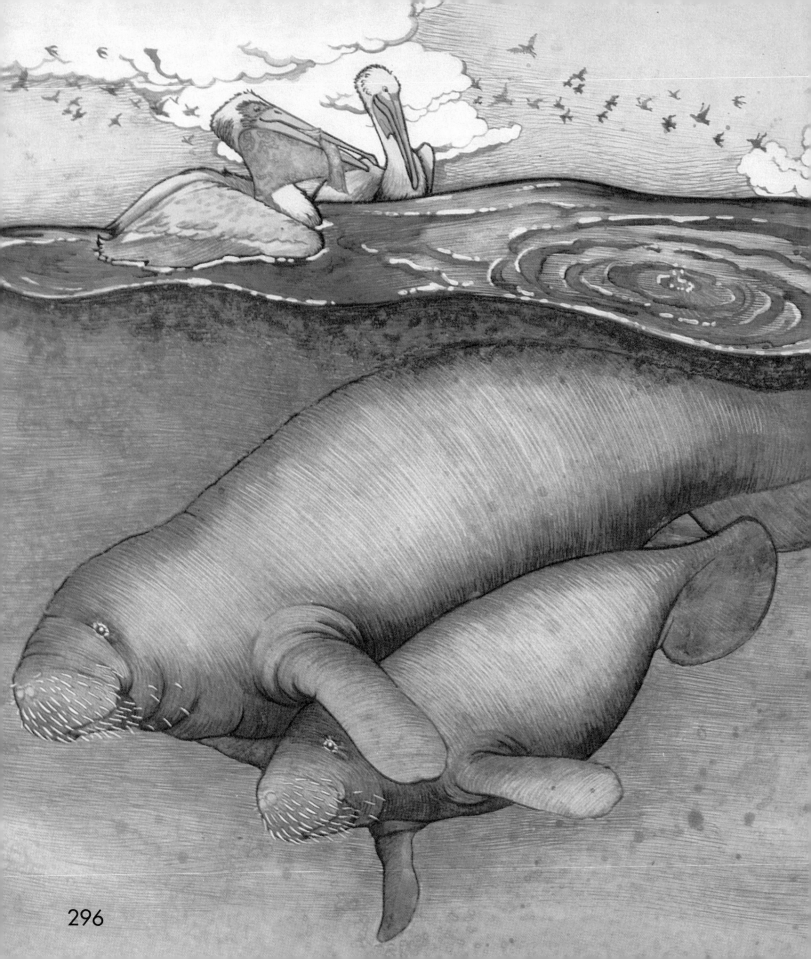

Aah-shoo! He breathes out.
Even though a manatee lives in the water,
it breathes air just like you and me.

Minutes go by.
Sam stays on his mother's back.
She ducks him.
Blub! Blub! Blub!
He bubbles.
Sam must hold his breath.
His mother lifts him into the air again.
Shoof-of! He snorts, happy for a breath.
His mother ducks him once more.
They practice this way until Sam
breathes in the air and
holds his breath underwater.

Manatees nurse their young in the water.
Sam finds a place beneath his mother's flipper
when he is hungry.
He sucks her warm milk.
Manatees are mammals like whales and dolphins.
Mammals feed their babies milk from special
parts of their bodies called mammary glands.

Sam follows his mother.

She swims with her big tail.

It is round and flat like a paddle.

Up and down it goes.

Sam swims with his two flippers.

They are shaped like mittens.

He will learn to use his tail later.

Sam looks like his mother.

He has little, round eyes and a small head.

He hears sounds

but he has no outside ears.

Sam's body is almost hairless.

It is shaped like a big pear.

CHAPTER

Sam stays near his mother for months.

But one day Sam hears a strange noise.

Gr-r-r-r-r-r-r-r-r.

Sam is curious.

He lifts his head to look.

But he can't see far, not more than a foot.

Eep! Eep! Eep! His mother squeals to warn him.

BAM!!

Too late! A motorboat hits Sam. The propeller cuts him.

Sam tumbles over and over.

Surely he will drown . . . but

his mother catches him just in time.

She lifts him up to breathe.

Motorboats are manatees' worst enemies.

Luckily, Sam's skin is thick and tough.
His wound heals but leaves a scar between his eyes.
It will be there for the rest of his life.

Sam and his mother swim out to the sea.
Months go by.
It is fall.
They move back up a river to warmer waters.
Mangrove trees grow thickly along the banks.
Small, silvery mullet fish
leap in front of them.
Alligators snooze on the shore.
Long-legged herons wade in the mud.

Sam is old enough now to eat plants
like other manatees.
He finds a bed of water hyacinths.
Ummmmmmm!
They taste good.
Manatees graze on floating hyacinths
like cows in a pasture.
Sam pokes his whiskered face into the plants.
He tugs at them with the two sides
of his divided upper lip.
He pulls them into his mouth.
Munch! Munch! Munch!
His flat teeth crush and grind the hyacinths.

Sam needs lots of plants to feed
his growing body.
He eats many pounds of plants each day.
Sam gets rounder and bigger.

Sam rests when he is tired.
He floats near the surface
or lies on the river bottom.
But he can't stay down more than five minutes.
He must come up to breathe.
Sometimes Sam pops up near
fishing boats and surprises the fishermen.

CHAPTER

Sam leaves his mother when he is two years old.
He goes off on his own.
Like other manatees, he spends the next few years
swimming along the seacoast in the warm months
and returning to the rivers in the cooler season.
When Sam isn't eating,
he goes exploring.
He swims around wooden pilings.
He searches under old piers.
He squeezes his big body through narrow places.

One day Sam swims off into a canal.

He finds a new place to explore.

It is a big, round cement pipe.

He flips his tail. He pushes with his flippers.

He wiggles and twists. He squirms half in.

But then he can't get out again.

Sam is stuck in a sewer drain.

People hear Sam's cries.

He is bruised, bleeding, and weak.

They try to help him, but Sam is too big.

Sam is nine feet long. He weighs as much as eight people.

Sam can't be moved from the drain.

So there he stays—half-in, half-out.

He gets hungry and grows weaker.

More people come.

Boys and girls run to see the stuck manatee.

Newspaper people come too.

But no one can budge poor Sam.

They call the Seaquarium.

Men come with trucks.

They pull Sam out of the sewer drain and

onto a stretcher.

A crane lifts the stretcher

and lowers Sam carefully onto a padded truck.

It will take Sam to the Seaquarium.

The newspaper people call him Sewer Sam.

"Good-bye, Sewer Sam!"

the boys and girls call.

Sam has a new home now.

He lives in a round, cement pool.

Keepers care for Sam.

They feed him lettuce leaves and bananas.

Soon Sam is feeling well again.

He swims around and around the pool.

But there is nothing for him to explore here.

Visitors come to the Seaquarium.

They come to see the killer whales
dance on their tails.

They come to see the dolphins
jump through hoops.

They come to see the sea lions
catch and balance balls.

Hardly anyone comes to see Sam.

Sam cannot do any tricks.

CHAPTER

A year passes slowly. The keepers think Sam is lonely.
They put him in another pool so he can have company.
Two other manatees live there.
Sam follows them around and around.
But they are happy together, and they don't want Sam.
Poor Sam!
The keepers finally decide to return him to a river.
But they worry.
Will Sam remember how to live in a river
after so much time in the Seaquarium?

The keepers slip a stretcher under Sam.
They fold his flippers in so they won't get hurt.
Sam is lifted out of the pool and into a soft, padded box.

He is covered with moist cloths.

"Good luck, Sam. We'll miss you," a keeper calls.

Sam is lifted to a truck and taken to an airplane.

The pilot flies Sam to Crystal River,

six hundred miles away.

Many manatees spend the winter

in the warm waters there.

Sam has never flown before.

But he is calm and still, even when he is sprayed

with water to keep his skin wet.

Sam is lowered into the water.

Men in rubber suits help Sam out of the box.

They swim with him, but Sam tries to hide

from them in a clump of weeds.

What's this? Food?

Munch! Munch! Munch!

Sam eats the weeds.

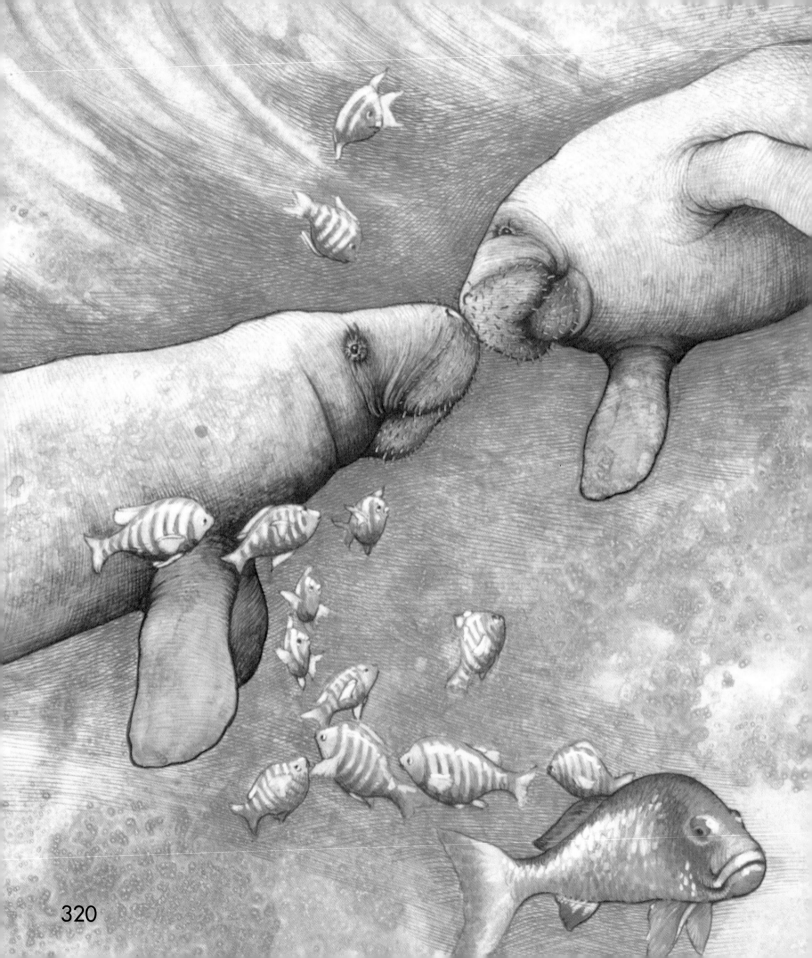

Days pass.

The men watch over Sam.

He seems happy to be free again.

Other manatees are swimming in the river.

Eep! Eep! Eep!

Sam calls them.

He flips his tail and swims to them.

One manatee turns to face Sam.

He puts his snout right up to Sam's.

They rub noses.

They rub whiskers.

The manatees begin to twist and roll.
They pop up and down.
They play follow-the-leader.
They swim off together.

Good-bye, Sam!

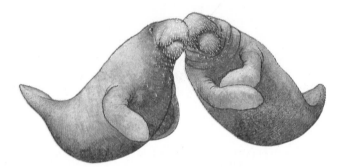

• What surprising things did you find out about manatees?

• Choose another animal that Sam is like. How is he like this animal? How is he different?

• How can people help keep manatees safe and healthy?

WRITE Pretend that you are Sam. Write a thank-you note to the keepers who let you go. Tell them what your life is like now.

Earth Partners

How are whales and manatees alike?

How did people in both stories show that they were "earth partners" with Ibis and Sam?

WRITER'S WORKSHOP

What can we do to help keep our water clean and safe for animals like Ibis and Sam? Make a poster about one of your ideas. Use the poster to make your classmates think that your idea is a good one. You might want to display your poster in your school or neighborhood.

CONNECTIONS

Multicultural Connection

Class Quilt

In the past, very little was thrown away. Clothes were worn until they were almost rags. The rags were then used to make warm and handsome quilts.

African American women made many of these quilts. Some of these women were artists who broke the old rules of quilt-making by making new patterns. Today some of their quilts are found in museums.

Quilts often tell a story about the quilt makers. Make a class quilt out of paper. Draw one square that tells a story about you. Then tape your square to your classmates' squares to form a quilt. Take turns telling about your own quilt square.

Social Studies Connection

Gifts from Throwaways

With a group, list things that people throw away. Then think of useful gifts that might be made from each of the things. Choose one of the gift ideas and write directions telling how to make it.

Art Connection

Recycled Art

Create a work of art with things that have been thrown away. You might glue what you find to cardboard, stick it into clay, or hang it from strings.

GLOSSARY

The **Glossary** can help you understand what words mean. It gives the meaning of a word as it is used in the story. It also has an example sentence to show how to use the word in a sentence.

The words in the **Glossary** are in ABC order. ABC order is also called **alphabetical order.** To find a word, you must remember the order of the letters of the alphabet.

Suppose you wanted to find *brilliant* in the **Glossary.** First, you find the **B** words. **B** comes near the beginning of the alphabet, so the **B** words must be near the beginning of the **Glossary.** Then, you use the guide words at the top of the page to help you find the entry word *brilliant.* It is on page 328.

A **synonym,** or word that has the same meaning, sometimes comes after an example sentence. It is shown as *syn.*

meaning

entry word — **bril·liant** Very bright: **The *brilliant* sunlight hurt my eyes.** *syns.* glowing, dazzling — example sentence

synonyms

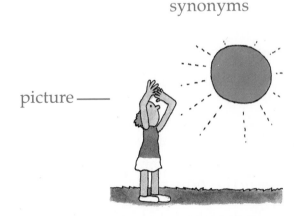

picture

A

angry

a·gainst   In the other direction; opposite: **Our team played** *against* **theirs last week.**

a·live   Living; not dead: **I was glad to see my bean plant was still** *alive* **after I forgot to water it.**

an·gry   Very mad: **Bobby was** *angry* **when his cat knocked the bowl off the table and broke it.**

an·noy   To make someone mad or unhappy: **Carmen hid my toy to** *annoy* **me.** *syn.* bother

ar·tist   A person who draws or paints: **The** *artist* **painted a picture of Mary's family.**

artist

a·shamed   Upset because you have done something that you think is silly, wrong, or not good enough: **I felt** *ashamed* **when I forgot Jim's birthday.** *syn.* embarrassed

a·void   To stay away from: **I walked the other way to** *avoid* **stepping into the puddle.**

aw·ful   Very bad: **Marco said the cake tasted so** *awful* **he couldn't eat it.**

B

brilliant

bor·ing   Not interesting: **The movie was so** *boring* **we fell asleep.** *syn.* dull

bought   Spent money to get something: **Daniela** *bought* **a book about horses with the money she had earned.**

bril·liant   Very bright: **The** *brilliant* **sunlight hurt my eyes.** *syns.* glowing, dazzling

brook   A small river. **We watched the little fish swimming in the** *brook*. *syns.* stream, creek

built   Made something; put something together: **My grandfather** *built* **the house we live in.**

C

cer·tain   Sure; not named but thought to be known: **There are** *certain* **people who are making too much noise in class!**

chance   A turn to do something: **Maria asked her teacher for a** *chance* **to answer the question.** *syn.* opportunity

change   To make or become different: **Minnie decided to** *change* **her drawing by adding a zebra to it.**

choose   To pick or select: **I had to** *choose* **between the red and the green lunch box.**

clev·er   Smart; good at doing things: **The** *clever* **girl helped the children learn the new game.**

coast   Land at the edge of the sea: **Cindy goes to the beach a lot because she lives on the** *coast* **of the Atlantic Ocean.**

coast

cour·age   Bravery when facing something dangerous or when afraid: **Sam showed** *courage* **when he saved the boy from drowning.** *syn.* heroism

cov·er   To hide or put on top of: **We will** *cover* **the chair with an old blanket when we paint the room.**

co·zy   Warm and comfortable: **I sit in my** *cozy* **chair by the fire on winter evenings.** *syn.* snug

cries   Loud shouts or calls: **We rescued the boys as soon as we heard their** *cries* **for help.**

cover

cu·ri·ous   Very interested to learn to know more: **Cats are so** *curious* **that they seem to want to find out about everything.**

D

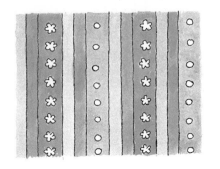

design

de·light·ed Very happy: **I was** *delighted* **to see my old friend.**

de·mand·ed Asked for very strongly: **The worker** *demanded* **that he be paid for his job.** *syn.* insisted

de·sign A pattern of form or color: **The wallpaper's** *design* **is made of colored stripes with white dots and flowers.**

dis·ap·pear To go away or become hidden: **We watched the plane** *disappear* **into the clouds.** *syn.* vanish

dis·tance A place far away: **I thought I saw Anna waving to me in the** *distance.*

dis·turb To bother or upset: **We hoped the squirrel would not** *disturb* **the birdhouse and cause the birds to leave.**

dye A liquid used to color cloth: **Kirby soaked the white shirt in purple** *dye* **to change its color.**

E

dye

ex·cit·ed Full of feeling: **Tammy is** *excited* **about having a new puppy.**

ex·plore To go into new or unknown places: **When the kittens got a little older, they left their familiar bed to** *explore* **the rest of the house.**

F

fi·nal·ly At last: **Mark** *finally* **earned enough money to buy a bicycle.**

fin·ished   Done: **My homework is** *finished,* **so now I can go out and play.**

fla·vor   The seasoning of food; taste: **I like the** *flavor* **of chocolate.**

fol·low   To come after or behind: **We watched the little ducks** *follow* **their mother as she led them through the water.**

follow

forced   Made someone do something: **The cold** *forced* **me to wear my mittens.**

fought   Tried very hard: **The butterfly** *fought* **to get out of the net.**

fu·ri·ous   Very angry: **Jan was** *furious* **when a bully picked on her little brother.**

G

guest   A person who is invited to stay or eat with someone else: **Max cooked dinner for his** *guest.* *syn.* visitor

guest

H

harm·less   Causing no harm or damage: **Most snakes are** *harmless* **to people, and they are more afraid of us than we are of them.**

I

in·gre·di·ents   Things listed in a recipe that are mixed together to make something: **Flour and sugar are two** *ingredients* **in cookie dough.**

ingredients

331

K

keen   Sharp; very strong: **Dogs have a** *keen* **sense of hearing that allows them to hear things people can't.**

light

L

larg·er   Bigger: **The balloon got** *larger* **and** *larger* **until it popped!**

light   **1** The opposite of *darkness:* **At night when it is dark, we still get** *light* **from the moon and stars.**
2 To cause to burn or give off light; to turn on: **Dad used matches to** *light* **the candle.**

light·ning   A sudden flash of light in the sky that happens during a storm: **The** *lightning* **lit up the sky during the storm.**

live·ly   Active; full of life: **The teacher smiled at the** *lively* **children running and shouting on the playground.**

lightning

M

ma·te·ri·al   Cloth: **Jan bought blue** *material* **to make a dress.** *syn.* fabric

meas·ured   Used the exact amounts as directed: **Tanya carefully** *measured* **one teaspoon of baking powder and added it to the mixture.**

mem·ber   One that belongs to a certain group: **The tiger is a** *member* **of the cat family.**

milk   A white liquid food that baby animals get from their mothers' bodies: **Newborn lambs drink their mothers'** *milk.*

material

N

noise   A loud sound: **Did you hear the loud** *noise* **the box of dishes made when it fell?**

P

paint·ings   Completed pictures done with paint: **In the museum we saw many** *paintings* **by famous artists.**

pres·ent   A gift; something nice that a person gives someone: **Everyone who came to Jim's party brought him a birthday** *present.*

pro·tect   To keep from harm: **I put on mittens to** *protect* **my hands from the cold.** *syn.* guard

R

reach   To stretch out to touch or take something: **Mrs. Jackson stood on tiptoe to** *reach* **the chain on the light.**

re·ceived   Was given; got: **I** *received* **a bicycle for my birthday.**

rec·i·pe   A list of ingredients and directions for making a food: **Please help me find the** *recipe* **for cornbread.**

S

scis·sors   A tool with two blades used for cutting: **I cut the paper in half with my** *scissors.*

noise

present

reach

sea·son   A particular time of year: **Panama and many other warm, tropical countries have a rainy** *season* **and a dry** *season.*

se·lects   Chooses; picks out: **Before he starts to draw, George** *selects* **his favorite crayons.**

sense   Reasonable meaning: **I like your idea because it makes** *sense.*

sew·ing   Making clothing and other things by using a needle and thread: **Mrs. Metz enjoys** *sewing* **pretty dresses for her granddaughter.**

supper

stretch·ing   Making longer: **We saw the giraffe** *stretching* **its neck to eat the leaves on the tree.**

sup·per   Dinner; a meal eaten in the evening: **Our family eats** *supper* **together every night.**

sup·pose   To imagine or believe that something is true: **I** *suppose* **you're hungry, since you haven't eaten all day.** *syn.* guess

sur·face   The top of the water, where the water meets the air: **When Manuel swims underwater, he comes up to the** *surface* **to breathe.**

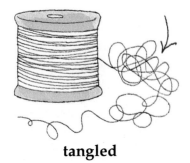

tangled

T

tang·led   Twisted and trapped: **The small butterfly could not escape because it was** *tangled* **in the net.**

taste   **1** Flavor; what makes food different and special in your mouth: **I love the** *taste* **of fresh strawberries.**
2 To take a bite: **Let's** *taste* **the stew to see if it needs more salt.**

them·selves   Their own selves: **The children looked at** *themselves* **in the big mirror.**

thor·ough·ly   Completely; without skipping anything: **Mom told us to clean our rooms** *thoroughly.*

throwing

throw·ing   Tossing: **Let's practice** *throwing* **the baseball.**

tough·er   Stronger; harder: **If you go barefoot on the beach a lot, the bottoms of your feet will get** *tougher* **than they are now.**

trou·ble   Difficulty; problem: **The bike caused Tonia** *trouble* **because the seat kept coming loose.**

tun·nels   Long, narrow spaces dug underground: **The ants dug** *tunnels* **in the ground in our backyard.** *syn.* passages

tunnels

V

va·ca·tion   A time away from the usual activities: **In July and August, we are out of school for the summer** *vacation.*

W

weath·er   The way things are outside: **I like the cool, dry** *weather* **in the fall.**

weave   To make cloth by lacing threads over and under each other: **I can** *weave* **pot holders on a little loom.**

weighs   Measures how heavy something or someone is: **My new baby brother** *weighs* **nine pounds right now.**

wool   The thick, soft hair taken from sheep or some kinds of goats and used to make clothing: **I wear sweaters made from** *wool* **when it's cold outside.**

weave

Acknowledgments continued

Philomel Books: Thunder Cake by Patricia Polacco. Copyright © 1990 by Patricia Polacco.

Plays, Inc.: "Stone Soup" by James Buechler from *Dramatized Folk Tales of the World,* edited by Sylvia E. Kamerman. Text copyright © 1971 by Plays, Inc.

G. P. Putnam's Sons, a division of The Putnam & Grosset Group: Cover illustration by Kathleen Kuchera from *The Rooster Who Went to His Uncle's Wedding* by Alma Flor Ada. Illustration copyright © 1993 by Kathleen Kuchera.

Marian Reiner, on behalf of Lilian Moore: "Ants Live Here" from *I Feel the Same Way* by Lilian Moore. Text copyright © 1967 by Lilian Moore.

Scholastic Inc.: Ibis: A True Whale Story by John Himmelman. Copyright © 1990 by John Himmelman. *Tyrone the Horrible* by Hans Wilhelm. Copyright © 1988 by Hans Wilhelm.

Tambourine Books, a division of William Morrow & Company, Inc.: Cover illustration by James E. Ransome from *How Many Stars in the Sky?* by Lenny Hort. Illustration copyright © 1991 by James E. Ransome.

Walker and Company, 435 Hudson Street, New York, NY 10014: Sam the Sea Cow by Francine Jacobs, illustrated by Laura Kelly. Text copyright © 1979 by Francine Jacobs; illustrations copyright © 1991 by Laura Kelly.

Albert Whitman & Company: Cover illustration from *Two of Everything* by Lily Toy Hong. Copyright © 1993 by Lily Toy Hong.

Charlotte Zolotow: "So Will I" from *River Winding* by Charlotte Zolotow. Text copyright © 1970 by Charlotte Zolotow.

Photograph Credits

Key: (t) top, (b) bottom, (c) center.

Harvey Wang/Picture Group, 100(t); Dr. E.R. Degginger, 101(t); HBJ Photo, 206(t); Harcourt Brace & Company/Maria Paraskevas, 206–207(c); Envision, 207(all); Tom McCarthy/Transparencies, 324(t); Neena Wilmont/Stock Art Images, 325(b)

Illustration Credits

Key: (t) top, (b) bottom, (c) center.

Table of Contents Art

Thomas Vroman Associates, Inc., 4, 5, 6, 8, 9

Unit Opener Art

Thomas Vroman Associates, Inc., 10, 11, 102, 103, 208, 209

Bookshelf Art

Thomas Vroman Associates, Inc., 12, 13, 104, 105, 210, 211

Theme Opening Art

Joe Veno, 14, 15; Lane Yerkes, 44, 45; Robert Frank, 64, 65

Unit 2

Ben Mahan, 106, 107; Oki Han, 154, 155; David Wenzel, 178, 179

Unit 3

Ron Garcia, 212, 213; Mary M. Collier, 260, 261; Jeffrey Greene, 278, 279

Theme Wrap-up Art

Thomas Vroman Associates, Inc., 43, 63, 99, 153, 177, 205, 259, 277, 323

Connections Art

Gordon Dunlap, 100, 325; Sue Parnell, 101; Gerald McDermott, 206; Lynn Rowe Reed, 324, 325

Selection Art

Adrienne Kennaway, 16–29; Shel Silverstein, 42; Olive Jar Productions, 46; Steven Kellogg, 47–60; Simms Taback, 62; Bernard Most, 66–81; Hans Wilhelm, 82–98; Frane Lessac, 108–124; Demi, 156–169, 172–175; Keith Baker, 180–193; Douglas Gutierrez and Maria Fernandez Oliver, 194–204; Nancy Winslow Parker, 214–238; Charles Schulz, 239; Patricia Polacco, 240–256; Marilyn Hafner and Darrin Johnston, 257; Jennifer Hewitson, 262–263; Aurther Dorros, 264–276; John Himmelman, 280–291